SEVEN DAYS TO
Sex Appeal

Other Books by Eva Margolies

Sensual Pleasure
The Best of Friends, the Worst of Enemies
The Samson and Delilah Complex
The Motherhood Report
Undressing the American Male
Men with Sexual Problems and What Women Can Do to Help

Other Books by Stan Jones

The Dynamics of Discussion: Communication in Small Groups
(with Dean Barnlund and Franklyn Haiman)
The Right Touch: Understanding and Using the Language of Physical Contact

SEVEN DAYS TO
Sex Appeal

Eva Margolies
and Stan Jones

Andrews McMeel
Publishing, LLC

Kansas City

08 09 10 11 12 WKT 10 9 8 7 6 5 4 3 2 1

ISBN-13: 978-0-7407-6069-3
ISBN-10: 0-7407-6069-6

Library of Congress Control Number: 2006930699

Illustrations by Neil Jeffery
Design by Holly Camerlinck

www.andrewsmcmeel.com

ATTENTION: SCHOOLS AND BUSINESSES
Andrews McMeel books are available at quantity discounts with bulk purchase for educational, business, or sales promotional use. For information, please write to: Special Sales Department, Andrews McMeel Publishing, LLC, 4520 Main Street, Kansas City, Missouri 64111.

To Steven.

—*Eva*

To Trevor, Chris, Natalya, Jonathan, and Teresa.

—*Stan*

Acknowledgments

We would especially like to acknowledge the pioneering scholarship of Albert Scheflen (for his courtship studies), Ray Birdwhistell (for his observations on gender displays), Paul Ekman (for his studies of facial expression and nonverbal leakage), Monica Moore (for her field studies of courtship patterns in women), Timothy Perper (for his discovery of the courtship sequence), and Helen Fisher (for her anthropological investigations of the biology of love).

There are many people without whose help this book would never have come to fruition. First, we thank Jody Rein for her effort in finding the right home for the book. We would also like to thank Chris Schillig, Caty Neis, and the staff at AMP for their enthusiastic support all along the way. AJ was responsible for the title so, thank you.

Steven, thank you for your patience. Ruth, we thank you for the many versions of this that you typed. Karen, thanks for your help with the manuscript. Chris and Natalya, we offer you a special thanks for the photos that served as the model for the illustrations. And Teresa, just thanks.

Finally, we thank the women and men we have had the privilege of coaching and making sexier.

Contents

One Preface
You Don't
Want to Miss!

This book will teach you how to enhance your sex appeal. If you follow our instructions, we guarantee you will have greater sex appeal, and you will see the positive effects right away—as soon as you begin to use the book. How can we make this claim?

First, this book is backed by our research, begun over six years ago, in which we discovered the key to sex appeal. Specifically, we made close observations of women and men in a variety of situations wherever sex appeal would be especially important. For example, we went into bars where singles hang out to discover which female signals attracted males. We also studied many hours of videotape, including movies in which sexy characters were depicted by cinema stars known for their sex appeal. What we found out was that women who have sex appeal are those who know how to effectively use female *gender signals,* the body-language behaviors that communicate feminine allure. As the introduction explains, these gender signals consist of the ways that a feminine woman moves her body and uses her eyes and voice to create an image—a set of qualities that anthropologists have identified as being sexually attractive to a man. These signals are not innate; they are learned, and you can learn to use them more effectively.

A second reason we can promise you more sex appeal as you read and use this book is that we have proven the practical value of our discoveries by extensive work with clients who have taken our Sex Appeal Coaching workshops, a training method involving role-playing and video playback. We have followed up with all of our clients, who consistently report dramatically improved success with potential romantic partners and better relationships with people in general. To learn more about our workshops, you can check out our Web site at www.sexappealcoaching.com. How does this coaching method relate to this book? In fact, through a story and artist's illustrations, we will show you exactly what coaching sessions look like, and you can practice the behaviors yourself as you read along. Think of us as your coaches.

The story format of this book is unique. Rather than providing long lists and descriptions of behaviors, the book will take you through the sex appeal coaching process, allowing you to imagine yourself experiencing the power of the coaching firsthand. The story is told in first person as a dialogue between author Eva Margolies, in her professional role as a sex appeal coach, and her client, Sally, a pretty woman who nevertheless lacks much sex appeal. Coauthor Stan Jones will make appearances in the later chapters to participate in the coaching process. Both authors are presented in caricature form in the story.

In the story, after Eva explains the principles behind sex appeal coaching to Sally in the introduction, she then gives Sally seven coaching lessons, each with a focus on a different set of gender signals—the "seven days to sex appeal" of the book title. In the epilogue, several months after Sally has completed the seven sessions, she comes back to report on her successes and receives additional instruction on how to handle sex appeal in the workplace. (Take a look at the contents to see the topics for each session.)

Is there a real "Sally"? Actually, there are a number of them, although none of them is named Sally in real life. However, the story line is realistic since it is based on our extensive coaching experience.

Our *strong recommendation* is that as you read each chapter, you practice the behaviors you see Sally learning. You may wish to read an entire chapter before going back to practice signals, or you may want to interrupt your reading to try each behavior after you have just seen Sally do it. A mirror will be sufficient to see how you look for most of the exercises. If you have access to one, a video recorder would be helpful, especially when the lesson, such as the one on walking, involves movement. An audio recorder would come in handy in "Day Five" where use of the voice is discussed. In the last chapters on flirting, a first date, and workplace sex appeal, it would be helpful to have a role-playing partner. This could be a guy friend, or it could be another woman (women are very good at playing the role of guys!).

You may find that just reading some chapters will allow you to make some positive changes in your behavior. This is most likely to be true if you feel you already have a fair amount of sex appeal and just wish to polish your image a bit. If you find that certain topics interest you more than others, you may be tempted to jump ahead to a chapter like "Day Six" on flirting and reading male signals, but you will better understand how Sally got to the skill level she shows at that point if you read the book straight through. In any case, we recommend you practice the behaviors physically as well as reading about them. As Eva explains to Sally in the introduction, it is important to get the new behaviors "into your muscle memory." Eventually you will want to practice the signals in real-life situations. It's important not to get discouraged if you don't have immediate success. Remind yourself, "It's just practice!" The positive results will come in the long run.

One special feature of this book is the "boxes" that provide additional information about sex appeal from scientific research and useful ideas for improving your image presentation. They offer details on such subjects as why smiles make everybody happy (including the person smiling), tips on grooming and jewelry, and lessons on how and when to touch a potential romantic partner.

Although you will meet your authors in caricature form in the story, we should introduce ourselves here so you will know our credentials. Eva Margolies holds master's degrees in communication and sociology, is a certified sex therapist, the owner of the Center for Sexual Recovery in New York, and the president of a consulting firm, Success Unlimited, Inc. She is the author of six previous books. Stan Jones, Ph.D., is Professor Emeritus of Communication at the University of Colorado in Boulder. He is an internationally recognized authority on body language and the author of more than twenty-five academic books, monographs, and articles.

We especially enjoy coaching. It's fun! We feel confident you will love reading this book and practicing the exercises. We'll be with you every step of the way!

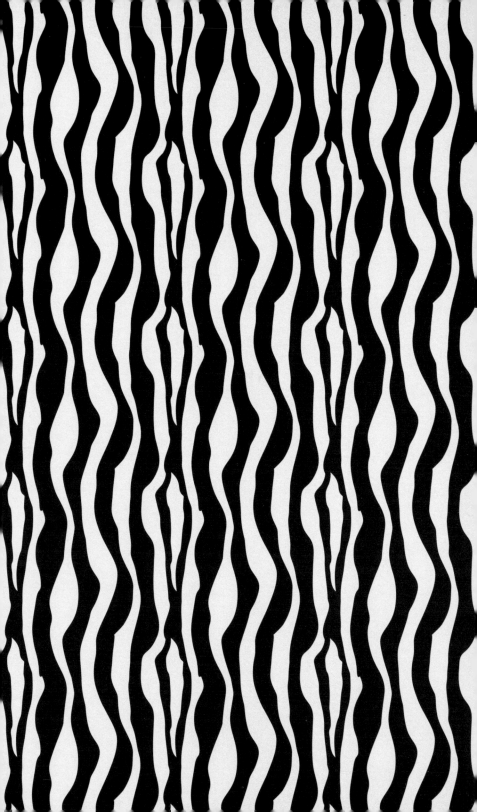

The Secret of
Gender Signals

It was payback time. Early in my career as a sex therapist and sex appeal coach, a savvy friend had spent endless hours teaching me everything I needed to know about making television appearances—what styles and colors to wear, the art of applying makeup for the camera, how to make curly hair look tame. She did not charge me, but we agreed that there would be a time in the future when I could reciprocate in my own way. When she called me about a friend of hers, we both knew this was the perfect opportunity.

"My friend Sally really needs your help," Katie told me. "Her boyfriend broke up with her six months ago, so her self-esteem is at an all-time low. And to be honest, even though she's pretty, she doesn't do too well attracting men."

"Of course I'll help," I offered immediately.

"I knew you would," she said. "But when I told her about the sex appeal coaching you and Stan have been doing around the country, she got very uptight. So I thought that instead of having her come to your office the first time, you could maybe just meet for coffee and explain what you do in a more relaxed atmosphere."

"I'll do the best I can," I told her.

The next day, Sally and I met at a sidewalk café near my office. She fit the description my friend had given me to a tee—tall, with legs up to her ears, pretty, but not the least bit sexy. She shook my hand limply and looked me over skeptically.

I purposely positioned myself in one of my more appealing poses and signaled for the waiter, who immediately came over.

"May we have menus, please?" I asked, darting my eyes in a sidelong glance and tilting my head ever so slightly. The waiter looked at me, then at Sally, and then back at me and smiled. Sally caught on.

"OK," she said. "How did you do that?"

"All in good time," I told her. "Why don't you tell me about yourself first?"

Sally sighed. "Look, I know that I'm pretty . . . prettier than a lot of women I know. The funny thing is that some of my less attractive friends definitely get more attention from men. They are also more successful at work. In fact, they seem to get more of a positive response from people in general."

"And why do you think that is?" I asked.

"I don't know! I guess that's why I'm here."

I smiled. "If you want me to, I'll teach you exactly what it is."

"OK." Sally smiled back.

"It's sex appeal," I said.

"Oh, no!" Sally looked crushed. "But you're either born with that or you're not! So I'll never attract a man."

"Of course you will," I laughed. "Sex appeal is something anyone can learn through coaching and practice. There are specific techniques that my colleague Dr. Stan Jones and I use that can transform people who don't have much sex appeal into people who are very sexually appealing. The techniques can also enhance the sex appeal of people who were already sexy."

"Techniques like wearing a dress cut down to your navel and up to your thighs?" Sally asked.

"Nope, unless all you want is to get sexual interest from a man."

"What about driving around in a fancy sports car?"

"Nope."

"What about having plastic surgery?"

"No! People are taking these drastic measures like getting surgery in order to be more physically attractive. And many of them could save a lot of pain and money if they heightened their sex appeal first, because sex appeal is not the same as physical attractiveness. Let's face it—you're prettier than many women are. But social scientists who have studied the subject have found that it's how often you use the signals that communicate sex appeal that determines how often men will approach you. So while prettier people may be the ones who are looked at first, as the party goes on, they are not the ones who are pursued the most."

"I don't understand. Are you saying that sex appeal has nothing to do with appearances at all?" Sally asked.

"It has a lot to do with appearances, but not in the way you think. Sex appeal has more to do with how men and women sit, stand, walk, and dress and the way they use their hands, voice, and facial expressions than it does with physical beauty."

"So sex appeal is about body language?"

"Yes, but the key to sex appeal is learning to effectively use a very special type of body language."

A guy on a motorcycle drove by and stopped at the light near the corner where we were sitting. An attractive blonde was crossing the street, and he gave her the once-over, let out a cat whistle, and licked his lips. Sally rolled her eyes.

"Then again, maybe it's a good thing to not have sex appeal," Sally said, both envious of the attention the blonde had received and at the same time relieved that she had not been the target of this guy's glance.

"Sex appeal isn't something that you have or don't have," I explained. "It's something that you can turn on or turn off, or turn higher or turn lower, depending on the situation you're in. If you're walking down the street and don't want to be noticed, you'll want to turn the sex appeal off. At work, it's probably prudent to turn it down. But knowing how to use sex appeal is valuable in so many areas of life, and people who know how have a definite advantage over people who don't."

We continued to talk long after our lunch plates had been removed. Sally was still uncertain. She had trouble believing, as do many people, that sex appeal goes beyond the bedroom. But in fact, sex appeal is important in long-term relationships (it keeps the spark going), on the job (people with sex appeal appear more competent and confident), and even in same-sex friendships (sex appeal can have a halo effect, and again, a confident, friendly person is nice to be around).

I convinced Sally on those points, but we had yet to tackle the main issue. Sally brought us there.

"OK, I get that sex appeal is useful," she said, "but if it's not how you look, what is it?"

"A lot of women don't know what sex appeal is because it's not one thing, but an overall image."

"What image is that?"

"From the earliest times humans were on Earth, women who had certain qualities were more likely to find a mate and pass on their genes to the next generation (Helen Fisher, *Why We Love*, 2004). Men looked for women who were confident in their attractiveness so that they would be noticed and who were comfortable with other women so that they would not be lonely and look for other men when their men were out hunting. They also wanted women who exuded some vulnerability so that men felt strong around them and who were approachable and supportive so that they would be good mothers and companions. Of course, they also wanted women who were interested in sex so that they could mate."

"You mean to tell me that men are still responding like cavemen?" Sally said, with more than a little irritation.

"I know," I told her. "In this modern day, it can seem strange that the driving force behind sex appeal is still reproduction. According to people who study the biological forces behind human behavior, men in all cultures still look for these qualities in women even today, although their motivations are largely unconscious."

"It sounds like a step back for the women's movement to me," Sally said.

"I totally understand. A lot of women Stan and I teach feel exactly the same way at first. But the fact of the matter is that you can combine being assertive with being feminine. It's a very powerful combination. Remember when I told you a few minutes ago that sex appeal can be helpful on the job? Well, it's true. Women who appear more feminine do better on the job than women who appear less feminine. It's not that women need to be extra vulnerable and sexy to be effective at work, although having attractive body language doesn't hurt as long as it's not overdone. Women have a number of special qualities like supportiveness and approachability that help them get ahead at work."

Sally softened a bit. She then asked the jackpot question. "Assuming I'm willing to go along with the idea of this image you say is appealing, what exactly am I supposed to do to project that image?"

"The answer is by learning to effectively use what are called *feminine gender signals*, the special body language behaviors that communicate the traits men find appealing. All women sit, walk, look at others, smile sometimes, and touch themselves. But it is *how* women do these things that communicates how feminine

The Effects of Feminine Gender Signals on Men

Research by psychologist Monica Moore, in a 1985 study in *Ethnology and Sociobiology*, found that women who displayed more feminine gender signals, regardless of the situation, received more signs of interest from men, either in the form of an approach or, after an approach, signals from the man showing attraction (moving in, touching, and so on). Women exhibiting signals more than thirty-five times per hour were approached or received signs of interest more than four times per hour; women who used ten or fewer gender signals were contacted only once in two hours.

In addition to smiling, some of the most effective female signals are:

Looking at the man and glancing away, or holding his gaze a few seconds: 9.68 approaches or signs of interest per hour.

Solitary *dancing* to music: 7.23 approaches/signs per hour.

Tossing her head and running her fingers through her hair: 6.89 approaches/signs per hour.

Licking her lips or touching her hair, clothing, or objects in a slow, sensual way: 4.4 approaches/signs per hour.

they appear. While there are other things women can do to look attractive, without knowing how to use gender signals appropriately, no one can be sexy."

"So you're saying that I don't have to act like some ditz to attract a man, but that I need to be better at using the gender signals that communicate the feminine traits that men find attractive?" Sally asked, feeling more comfortable.

"That's exactly right. And anyone can learn these gender signals with practice. If you give me a week, I can teach you most everything you need to know."

Sally seemed skeptical. "It sounds almost miraculous."

"Not at all," I reassured her. "In fact, you use gender signals in things you do every day: sitting, standing, walking, using your hands, using facial expressions, and getting dressed. So all you need to do is practice what you usually do, except in a more sexually appealing way.

"I'll tell you what," I continued. "Seeing is believing. So come to my office tomorrow, and I'll give you your first lesson, and you'll see for yourself how easy it is."

"OK, I'll be there," Sally responded. "I have a blind date tonight, so I'll see what happens."

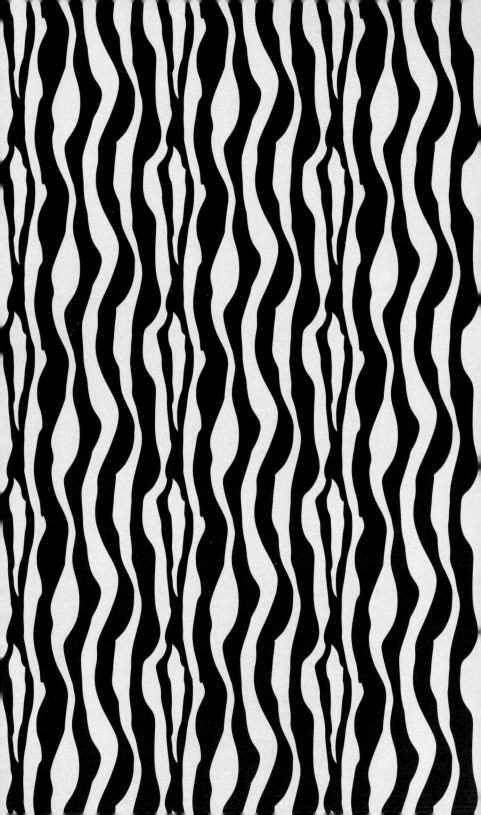

Sexy Ways
of Sitting

Sally looked excited and nervous sitting in the reception area of my office. It is always interesting to assess how much sex appeal a client has and to imagine how much she will have after she finishes the coaching. As I walked toward Sally, I could see immediately that there were a lot of things we would need to work on, and that when we were done, she was going to be very sexy.

"Hi," I said, greeting her with a smile and pointing toward my office. "Why don't you go back and make yourself comfortable? I'll be with you in a moment." Sally did not know that I wanted to watch her walk. What she also did not know was that the video camera in the office was running.

When I walked in, Sally settled into my large, cushiony couch and sat in a way that women who do not have a lot of sex appeal often do: She plopped down, her legs were together at the knees, almost knock-kneed, and her feet sprawled out to each side. It was not in the least bit sexy.

"So how did your date go last night?" I asked, sitting across from her and out of view of the camera.

"I thought it was going well. It seemed like we had a good conversation with good eye contact. So I thought he was interested." Sally sighed. "At the end of the evening, he said I was nice but he just didn't feel any chemistry. So I'm clueless about how to figure out if a guy's interested short of his jumping my bones and even more clueless about what I'm doing wrong."

"Maybe you'll be able to figure it out after watching this." I got up, walked over to the corner, and shut off the video camera that had been camouflaged by some large plants. "I've been videotaping you," I told her.

Sally was mortified.

"One of the best ways to see what you're doing wrong is to see how others see you," I continued. "So let's watch."

I waited a few minutes so that Sally could get over the narcissistic shock of seeing herself, a common reaction that almost everyone has when first viewing themselves on camera. "So what do you notice?" I finally asked.

"Well, my hair's a mess. . . . I look fat. . . . ," she said

Sally's slumping posture is a dead giveaway to her lack of confidence.

self-consciously. I didn't know that learning sex appeal meant being videotaped," she said, shooting me an anxious, skeptical look.

"Almost everyone has the same reaction to seeing themselves at first," I reassured her. "It will get easier after you watch for a few minutes. So look again and tell me what else you see. Specifically, I want you to look at your body language."

Sally looked closely at the frame that was on the screen. "I don't look very confident," she said finally.

"What makes you say that?"

"I'm slouching. It almost looks like I have no boobs."

"Or that you're ashamed of them," I added. "And you're right. You don't look confident in yourself or your appearance, and both of these qualities are important in communicating sex appeal."

Sally looked slightly offended but curious.

"So I want you to try this while you watch yourself in the

monitor, and at home I'd like you to try this while looking in the mirror. Sit up straight with your shoulders back. Breathe through your diaphragm, because it's difficult to slouch when you're diaphragm is filled with air. I'll keep running the tape so that you can see yourself in the monitor."

Sally threw her shoulders way back and sat up very straight and stiff. She looked like a wooden soldier.

"Relax a little," I told her.

Sally shook some of the tension out of her body. Looking in the monitor, she saw that she already looked better.

"OK, now bring your chin up so that you look like you are holding your head up high."

Sally tried, but after a few seconds, she started to lower her head and slouch. "The truth is," Sally said in a hushed voice, "I don't really feel all that confident."

"I know—a lot of women feel the same way," I told her. "That's the beauty of this method of learning sex appeal. You don't need to feel

When You're Doing This, Think About . . .

Expand your diaphragm fully as you breathe. That will make it impossible for you to slouch.

Take in the world around you with your eyes. That will help you to keep your chin up.

Think about something you have done that you feel proud of. Your posture will automatically reflect what is in your mind.

Sally begins to transform herself as she sits up straighter and suddenly looks more self-assured.

confident to practice looking confident. And that's what you need to do—practice, practice, and practice. Over time, these new ways will get into your muscles and feel more natural. It's called *muscle memory*. The best part is that once it's in your muscles, not only will you *look* more confident, but you will also *feel* more confident."

"So you're saying that if you change the way you use your body, the way you feel will change also."

"Exactly."

After a few minutes of practicing and watching herself, Sally found it easier to sit in a more confident pose. She took a look at herself again, this time in a nearby mirror.

"That looks good," I told her. "Now let's work on what to do with your legs."

"What's wrong with my legs?" Sally asked. She was sitting with one leg on the ground and the other with her ankle on her knee.

"Nothing, if you only want to look professional. But if you notice, men sit in a similar way, so it just doesn't look very sexy."

Sally frowned. She was beginning to feel like nothing she was doing with her body was correct. "Are you telling me this is a masculine way to sit? Because I see a lot of women sitting this way," Sally asked a bit defensively.

"No, it's not masculine, but it's not feminine either. It is more gender neutral. There's a secret to communicating sex appeal with your legs," I said, lowering my voice. "Taking up a lot of space with your legs is not sexy. Taking up a small amount of space with your legs while at the same time accentuating them is. I want you to try this."

I then asked Sally to reposition herself, sitting forward with her elbows on her knees and her legs spread apart. "How does it look if you sit like this?"

Sally laughed. "I'd look like a guy, unless I was wearing a skirt like you, and then I'd look like . . ." We both laughed.

"You're right. So I want you to try something. Try sitting with both legs up on the couch and position them so that they take up less space than if you were sitting cross-legged."

Sally pulled up both of her legs on the couch and tucked them under her body. Seeing her reflection in the monitor, she could see that she looked a bit more coy.

"Good!" I told her, excited as always to see someone change before my eyes. "Even better would be if you wrapped the ankle of your bottom leg over the top of the other ankle like a pretzel. That way, you're taking up even less space and exposing your ankle."

Sally tried it and could see what I meant.

"Now imagine that there is no couch but just a chair, and try taking up less space with your legs. First try without crossing them."

Sally learns the first rule about communicating sex appeal with her legs: Don't take up a lot of space and accentuate the curves.

Sally sat up straight with her knees together and legs planted firmly on the ground.

"Try again," I smiled. "You look like a schoolmarm. I'll give you a hint. Do something different with the angle of your legs."

Sally suddenly got up. "Aren't we going a bit far with the feminine thing?" she asked, sounding and looking annoyed. "I frankly would rather have a man not attracted to me than have him attracted to me because I'm doing the 'Look at me, I'm a hot babe' thing."

"You be the judge," I said calmly, having heard this objection before. "I want you to try sliding your legs to the left and hooking your right foot around your ankle."

Sally sat down again and unenthusiastically did what I suggested.

"OK, look in the monitor," I told her. "How do you think you look?"

"That does look more alluring," she admitted.

"It sure does. And it doesn't look ditsy at all. You may feel at first that you look silly or exaggerated because these behaviors are new to you. I guarantee that when you look at yourself, you'll still see yourself, but better—more confident and more sexy. Now I want you to try to take up less space with your legs while crossing them."

Sally crossed her right leg over her left, resting her arms comfortably on the top of her thigh.

"Good," I said approvingly. "But you'd look even sexier if you moved your top knee forward so that it is perched in front of your back knee. It shows off more of your leg."

Sally improves her pose by sliding her legs to the side and hooking one foot around the other ankle.

Sally watched me demonstrate and then slid her own knee forward, watching herself in the monitor. "It looks sexier when you do it because you're wearing a skirt," she commented.

"You're right," I admitted. "If you want maximum sex appeal, it's better to wear a skirt or dress, because it's easier to accentuate your legs. But even in slacks, you can look sexier by taking up less space when you sit and showing as much leg and ankle as you can."

"Now if you really want to look feminine," I added, "lace your fingers over your knee instead of resting them on your thigh."

Sally perches one knee over the other and laces her fingers in front to accentuate her sex appeal.

Sally leaned forward slightly and placed her hands so that they were holding her knee. She looked at herself in the monitor. She looked smaller in an alluring way, more feminine, and sexier. She was beginning to feel a little sexier, too.

"You're a good student!" I applauded. "There's one last thing you can do that is especially sexy to guys who like the delicate type. Pretzel your top leg around the bottom like this."

Sally watched as I twisted her upper calf around her lower calf, hooking her foot close to her lower ankle. "You have to be kidding," Sally said. Eventually, she maneuvered her body into the correct position, but she didn't feel very comfortable.

"Some women can't do that one. It's not critical, but just another potential way of presenting yourself. Remember, a lot of this will feel uncomfortable and unnatural at first," I said encouragingly. "So don't worry. As you keep practicing, it will seem more natural. You will also develop the repertoire of signals that feel most comfortable and suit you best."

"OK. There's one final thing you need to learn about looking sexy when you sit, and that is how you actually take your seat in the first place."

"Are you telling me I don't know how to sit down?" Sally asked, getting uptight again.

"Of course you do, but not in a sexy way. Stand up for a minute and then sit down again in this chair."

Sally did as I instructed and watched as I played back the tape.

"It just looks to me like I'm sitting down," she said, perplexed.

"That's the point. You don't want to just sit down, but

insinuate into the couch or chair. You also want to smooth your clothing over your derriere as you sit."

"I don't know what you mean by insinuating."

"When men sit down—let's say at a table in a restaurant—they may pull out the chair a little way and then step sideways until they are just over the seat before sitting down. But to look more appealing—hopefully while a man is holding the seat out for you, but even if he isn't—you want to slide into the seat sideways, bringing your legs in just afterward. Try it."

Sally sat down again, this time leading with her hip as she sat down. "I think I get it," she said. "It's almost like I'm gliding over the seat before the rest of my weight comes down. And I notice I can actually leave my legs slanted toward the side where I approached the seat—the sitting posture we worked on before."

"That's a good point," I said. "That emphasizes the curve of your body even more."

"Let's just go over what you learned today so that you can practice before we meet next," I told her, as a way of getting what she had learned into her muscle memory. "Look in the monitor as we review. It will help you to remember. At home, you can practice by looking in the mirror. First, stand up and insinuate yourself into the chair while smoothing your clothing down over your buttocks."

Sally giggled as she rehearsed this new way of looking demure.

"Now, in order to look more confident, sit up straight with your shoulders relaxed."

Sally adjusted her posture while watching herself.

"In order to look more alluring, you want to take up less

space with your legs. Put your legs out in front of you and wrap one foot around your ankle, which brings attention to your ankle."

Sally did as I suggested.

"Now cross your legs and push your top leg forward so that the top knee rests directly over the other knee, and point your toes slightly. This will make your leg look longer and draw more attention to it."

Sally crossed her legs and moved her top leg forward.

"You can also wrap your hands around your knee, which draws attention to your hands as well as your legs."

Sally readjusted herself quickly. "I feel like I'm starting to get this!" she said.

"You see! It gets easier the more you do it," I said, smiling. "That's it for today. Don't forget to practice! Tomorrow we'll be working on how to have a more appealing stance and walk. So please wear a skirt or dress and bring a pair of higher heels with you."

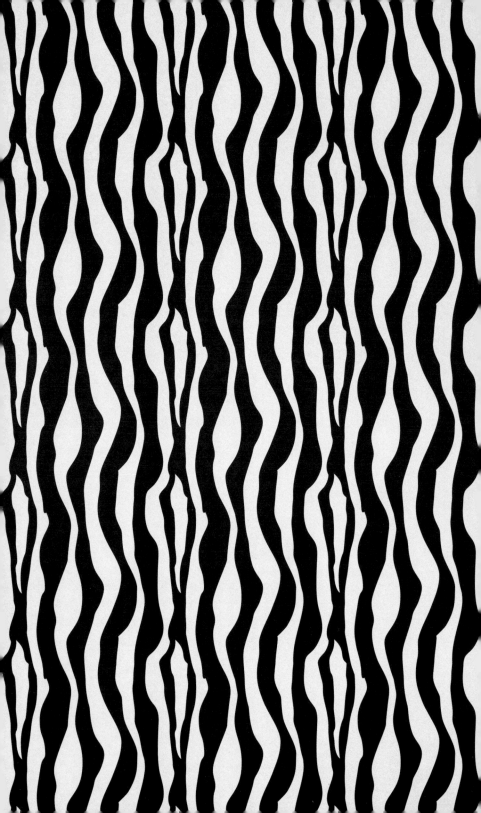

Sexy Stance
and Walking

When I greeted Sally in the reception area the next day, like most women after their first coaching session, she was already looking more appealing. She was sitting straighter. With her head held higher and her shoulders back, she looked more approachable and more confident, and having her legs slid to the side added a nice element of sensuality. The profound change in a woman's projection of herself as well as in her own body image after such a small amount of coaching never ceases to amaze and delight me.

After complimenting Sally, I mapped out the schedule for the day. "Today we are going to work on exuding sex appeal while standing and walking. There is good news and bad news. The good news is that once you learn these elements, the way you come across will be dramatically more appealing. You will look very different. The bad news is that today will probably be the longest and most difficult for you. That's because learning to walk in a seductive way not only takes time, but also you are likely to feel clumsy while you are learning it."

"I'm already frustrated because I feel like a sex appeal zero. Things like sitting and standing that I thought I should be able to do without thinking are now things I need to pay attention to," Sally said with a sigh. "I did spend some time watching women walk down the street after I left yesterday, and I have to admit that some women definitely move in a way that looks sexier."

"Why do you think there are so many songs about that, like the Beatles' 'Something' or Billy Joel's 'She's Got a Way'? A lot of a woman's attitude about sex and sensuality is reflected in the way she walks."

"OK, I'm game, although I have a concern."

"Shoot."

"The concern is that when I walk down the street, I don't want to turn every man's head, and that's the reaction that some of the women with the sexiest walks get."

"I understand what you're saying, although what you think men are thinking is probably not what they are actually thinking," I told her. "You're right that in some situations like being out on the street or at work, you will not want to stand and walk

Mind-Reading Mistakes

Women may think that a man is thinking:

"She must be a prostitute."

"Why is that slut flaunting herself like that?"

Examples of what men are actually likely to be thinking to themselves or saying for the benefit of male companions:

Humorous: "Shake it honey, but *please* don't break it!"

Admiration: "Now that is one sweet ass!"

Appreciation: "Lady, you just made my day!"

Envy and respect: If she's with a man, "Now there's a lucky man!"

in the same way as when you are trying to attract a man you're interested in. In addition to learning how to come across as sexier, you will learn how to turn the volume up and down at will. We will be starting with a basic appealing stance and walk that are appropriate in almost all situations, including work, and keep heating things up by adding more and more elements. So how far you go and how much attention you attract will be largely up to you."

"Are you saying that I get to control how much of a magnet I am?" Sally asked.

"That's exactly what I'm saying. It will become clearer in a moment. Let's start by reviewing the qualities that men find appealing in women and that we are going to work on teaching you to communicate with gender signals."

"I'm better prepared than when you tested me yesterday," Sally laughed. "First, men look for women who are confident in their appearance. I also want to come across as supportive and approachable, interested in sex, and a teeny bit vulnerable to bring out a man's rescue instinct, although I have no idea how I'm supposed to communicate these things with how I stand or walk."

"It's not as complicated as you think. Like sitting, a sexually appealing stance and walk for a female are almost the opposite of what they are for a male. A man wants to take up a lot of space when sitting and walking so that he can look powerful and strong. As a woman, you want to take up a smaller amount of space while still looking confident and emphasizing the curves of your body."

I then asked Sally to keep that in mind as well as the characteristics that men find sexually appealing and to stand up and face me as she would if the two of us were casually talking to each other on the street.

Sally stood erect, with one foot slightly in front of the other and with arms dangling down, her hands clasped loosely together in front of her body covering her pelvic region.

"OK, look at yourself in the monitor, and let's evaluate what you're doing."

"I'm not taking up much space, and my posture isn't bad," Sally said.

"That's true. But do you think you look confident?"

"Hmm, not really. I'm still slouching a little."

"Do you look approachable?"

Sally pondered this for a bit. Wanting to come across as approachable was important to her. "I don't look unapproachable," she said a bit defensively. "It's not like my hands are crossed over my chest."

"That's true," I told her. "But with your hands in front of your body, you don't look as open as you might, to say nothing of the fact that you are covering up your genitals."

"Isn't that psychobabble? Are you saying my unconscious is doing that?" Sally said defensively.

"It's hard to say for sure what your motivation is," I told her, "but to a man, it may look like you're covering up."

"Maybe you have a point," Sally said. "I guess people do respond subliminally sometimes."

"OK, let's keep looking. Do you look vulnerable?"

"Yes," she said, "but not in a particularly good way."

"You're right. You look insecure, which is not alluring, as opposed to confident and delicate, which is an attractive combination."

"I'm not exuding appeal at all," she said in a discouraged tone.

"No, you're not, but that is amazingly easy to fix. You can make a big difference in your stance simply by placing your hands behind you."

"Hmm," Sally nodded in approval as she observed herself in the monitor automatically clasping her hands behind her buttocks. She noticed immediately that with her hands behind her, she was standing taller, and her breasts protruded in an appealing and subtle way. "It looks one hundred times better this way," she said with a smile.

"That's because with your hands behind your back, you automatically are standing straighter, and subtly emphasizing some of those great curves. You could turn up the volume a bit more by pressing your hips forward. That's called *pelvic presentation*, and it adds another dimension to the basic stance."

Sally thrust her pelvis forward slightly and looked at her image. "It makes me look a little sexier, but it also makes me look a little more vulnerable, so I'm not sure if I like it."

"OK, let's go back to the basic sex appeal stance for now. I'd like you to do one more thing: Spread your legs apart so that your weight is equally balanced between the two feet, and place one leg in front of the other and turn your forward foot out so that it points away from the other foot."

Sally adjusted her stance. "Like a ballet dancer who is turned out?" she asked.

"That's right. Notice what this does with your weight distribution."

"My weight is now on my back leg."

"Exactly. Now look at what this stance automatically does to your left hip."

"My hip sticks out a little," Sally said, surprised at how such a subtle shift could make such a difference.

"This is called *hip presentation* because it emphasizes the curve of your hip."

The basic sexually appealing stance: open posture and subtle emphasis on breasts and pelvis.

"This stance looks good," Sally said approvingly.

"This is what I call the more powerful version of your *basic sex appeal stance*: erect posture, one foot forward and turned out so that your hip is projected slightly, and hands behind your back. It makes you look approachable and confident in your attractiveness. You also look like you are a sexual person, without being provocative. It's also a strong stance, so you can use it at work."

"I can see that," Sally said.

"Now, everything else we are going to add to these basic stances will turn up the volume by making you look either a little more vulnerable or a little to a lot more sexual. So when you practice, start with a basic stance and play around with the added dimensions. Let's start with your foot turned out again and have you cock your head slightly toward the hip side. That will expose the curve of your neck and make you look a little vulnerable."

Sally tilted her head first to the hip side, then toward her forward foot. "Does it really matter which side I tilt my head to?" she asked.

"Look at yourself doing it both ways, and tell me what you think."

Sally experimented in front of the monitor for a minute. "It looks more skeptical rather than sweet when I tilt it toward the forward foot," she said.

"Exactly."

"I really hate the vulnerable thing," Sally said.

"I know, but we're just experimenting right now. Just try it. By the way, a little smile wouldn't hurt."

Grudgingly, Sally tilted her head and forced a smile.

Why Is It Important to Men That Women Look a Little Helpless?

In her 2004 book *Why We Love*, anthropologist Helen Fisher points out that for millions of years, males have protected and provided for females. She says that there is abundant psychological research showing that men like to help women because men are inclined to be problem solvers, and both nature and nurture contribute to this.

What benefits do men get from rescuing women? First of all, it makes them feel strong and manly, fulfilling their testosterone-driven destiny. The giver must have a receiver to feel satisfied. Secondly, and more crucially, protecting gives men potential rights to a desirable female, including "protecting" her from other males. This relationship can be seen throughout the animal kingdom. Take elks, for example. During mating season, the strongest male maintains his harem of females by being a better protector than other males, who may be left without any females.

"How do you think that looks?"

"Not all that helpless," she admitted. "I look sweet and a little sexy."

"Yes, you do. You actually also look more approachable. Remember, you don't have to look like you can't fend for yourself for men to find you attractive. But it doesn't hurt to keep in mind that it boosts a man's ego to help a damsel in distress.

"OK, now let's spice it up a bit," I continued. "Remember, the way to add sex appeal to your stance is to emphasize your curves in as many ways as you can. Let's start by pressing your pelvis forward a little and accentuating your hip even more by placing your left hand on your left hip."

When You're Doing This, Think About . . .

A great way to remind yourself to stand in a more appealing way is to think of the letter S because of its curves. Emphasizing most any curve—a hip, a wrist, an ankle, a buttock, or a neck—will make your stance automatically more appealing.

Sally tilted her pelvis forward slightly and placed her hand around her hip, with her fingers together in front and the thumb in back, much the way guys do it.

Sally said, "It's almost like pointing to my pelvis and hip."

"Right, it's as though you're saying, 'Take a look at this, guys.'"

Sally looked at herself approvingly. "I like this stance because it looks sexy and assertive at the same time."

"Yes, it does. Actually, this is a good stance to use at work

Sally accentuates her curves with her hand position.

for exactly that reason. It looks appealing, approachable, and confident without looking vulnerable or delicate."

Sally started playing around a bit and put her other hand on her hip. "How about putting both hands on my hips?"

"That's called *arms akimbo*," I told her, "and the way you're doing it sends a confusing message—part sexy, but not at all

The Power of Pointing

In analyzing films and videotapes frame by frame, nonverbal communication pioneer scholar Albert Scheflen (*Human Territories*, 1976) made an interesting discovery. He found that people constantly use their hands, head and eyes, and even feet or torso to point toward things other people should notice. It's much subtler than pointing with the index finger. People do it by raising the chin in a certain direction, for example, as if to say to a companion, "Check that out over there!" In another situation, a woman may occasionally move her head and eyes around to take in surroundings while talking to a male who may be getting a little too flirtatious. The message: "Notice where we are—this is not appropriate in this social setting."

approachable or vulnerable. Try putting your feet apart with the weight balanced between them to get the full effect."

Sally spread her legs apart a bit more. "That looks really aggressive. Seems like it would scare a guy off or else make him aggressive in return."

"With the exception of the guy who's into being dominated, you're right. Remember, you want to emphasize your curves. That stance takes up too much space. Instead of emphasizing the hip, it draws attention to the shoulders and looks masculine. So let's go back to the original basic stance with just one hand on your hip."

I continued. "Now, if you want to turn up the volume and look more feminine, reverse your hand and put your thumb in front and fan your hand downward across your hip."

Sally switched the position of her hand.

"You see how this causes the wrist to bend more so that you see its curve? You look more delicate and sexy at the same time. You can also shift the position of your hand so that your fingers are fanning the top of your butt."

"I would never use this at work," Sally said.

"No, the volume is up too high in this case. But if you want to get male attention, this pose looks confident, sexy, and approachable. Let's go back to your hand on your hip with your thumb in front."

Sally realigned herself, right foot forward and pointed outward, with her hand fanning her left hip.

"There is one last variation. We've emphasized the neck, the hip, and a little bit of the butt. The final variation of the stance when you want to turn the volume up is to bring attention to the leg and the ankle. What I want you to do is to pull in the knee that is most forward—this time, make it your left knee—and turn it toward your other knee and turn your ankle in so that your ankle is exposed. You would not want to use this stance at work because it doesn't look like your feet are firmly planted, but it is a great look for attracting someone you're interested in."

Sally pulled in her leg and turned out her ankle. I could tell

that she felt a little awkward, although the truth was that she looked like a knockout. Sally sheepishly agreed.

"You don't think it's too much?" she asked a bit defensively.

I then instructed Sally to do what I advise all my clients when they feel that what they are doing with their bodies looks exaggerated. "Look at yourself as objectively as you can. Then ask yourself what you would say if you saw a woman looking like the image in the monitor."

Sally thought for a second and said, "I'd wish I looked like her."

"Great—that's what we're working toward! OK, let's review the stance quickly, and then we'll take a break. I'll do it with you. Start with the basic stance with good posture, one leg in front of the other with foot turned out and hands behind back. . . . Now cock your head slightly and put one hand on your hip with your thumb on your back and tilt your pelvis forward a bit.

"Looking good," I said encouragingly. "OK, now reverse your hand so that your thumb is pointing toward your butt, and then slide your hand down a bit so that you are almost patting your butt. . . . And last but not least, turn in your left knee and expose your ankle.

"Good work. Let's take a fifteen-minute break. Just so you know," I added, "I will be videotaping you as you walk so that we can review it when you get back."

As Sally left my office and walked down the long corridor, I changed the position of the camera to follow her so that I could record her walk as she left and when she returned. She walked like many people do, and like many women who do not feel confident: head down, eyes averted, shoulders hunched, and hips

moving front to back rather than side to side. This part of the coaching was definitely going to be the most challenging for Sally. Actually, it is for most women.

Sally seemed excited when she returned. "I went down to the coffee shop and practiced the basic stance, and two really cute guys looked at me," she said smiling. "I guess this stuff works!"

"I'm glad you're getting more comfortable with it," I told her. "OK, now let's get to work. We are going to work on a very important part of self-presentation—the walk. It's one of the most effective signals because, if done right, it gets attention and interest from men. I'm going to play back the tape of you walking, and I'd like you to tell me what you think," I said, turning on the tape.

"Why do you keep asking me what I think when you're the expert?"

"I want you to get used to viewing yourself objectively so that you can practice what you're learning more effectively and begin developing minor variations on your own. *You* need to get a sense of what is appealing or not and why or why not."

"OK," Sally said, observing herself, "I'll give it a shot." I rewound and replayed the tape so that she could see it.

"The walk is not sexy at all," she said without reproach. Sally was starting to get into more of an observer mode that allowed her to see what was happening more critically, without feeling ashamed or embarrassed—an important leap in the coaching process.

"I'm slouching, so I don't look at all confident in my attractiveness," she said. "I don't look at all approachable with my head bent forward. There's nothing feminine or sexy about the walk at all. What's surprising is that I think I look vulnerable, but not in a good way. I mean, I look so unalert that I almost look like an easy target, if that makes any sense."

"That's an astute observation. Many women think that the best way to avoid problems in a place like a city is to disappear. And while it's true that you will not attract male attention walking the way you do, you might look like an easy target for a mugger because you don't look alert. So even when you don't want to draw attention to yourself, it is important to look confident."

"That means stand up straight with head held high, right?"

"Exactly. Why don't you stand up so that we can start working on it? Walk down the corridor, but this time keep your head and chin up. Keep your gaze straight ahead so that you look like you are intent about where you are going."

Sally tried the walk and found it easy to accomplish.

When You're Doing This, Think About . . .

As you look at yourself in the mirror and evaluate how appealing you look, keep reminding yourself of the elements that communicate sex appeal. Do you look confident? Approachable and supportive? Interested in sex? A tiny bit vulnerable?

Answering "no" to any of these questions will give you an immediate clue about where to start correcting your behavior.

"This works well for walking down the street in the city because I look stronger and more confident without looking particularly provocative."

"True, but do you think it works as far as coming across as sexually appealing?"

"Not really," Sally admitted.

"Let's try something," I told her. "Imagine that the corridor is a bar and that you're going to walk past a line of men, some of them standing and some sitting, but all of them in a position where they could readily look at you if they chose to."

Sally looked flustered. "I feel really shy in that situation and would try to get it over with as quickly as possible."

"Just try it," I urged.

Sally walked down the corridor and past the imaginary bar in record time, with her head down and no particular hip sway. "You see, that's how I would do it. I know I should have better posture, but in that situation I feel like I would be flaunting myself, as if to say 'Come and get me!'"

"Not at all. You're just showing that you have self-esteem, that you're confident of your attractiveness and not afraid."

"I never thought about it that way."

"Let's work on this—social scientist Monica Moore called it the *parade walk*, and it's your basic appealing walk. It involves having good posture, keeping your chin up, and having a slight closed-mouth knowing smile, which will make you look a bit mysterious."

"Like I had great sex last night but I'm not talking," Sally said, understanding immediately.

"That's it exactly. OK, I want you to do several passes by the imaginary bar with this walk. Remember, stand straight, keep your head up, and smile with your mouth closed."

Sally watched herself do the walk on the monitor. She could see the effect, and the walk itself wasn't difficult. But she still felt extremely self-conscious.

"Now that wasn't so bad, was it?" I asked.

"The walk was easy, but I got really uptight imagining one of

The Double Edge of Attraction— Display and Mystery

Both men and women strut to get attention for courtship. Strutting for sexual interest is common in many animal species, but interestingly, it is more prevalent among males than females in most species. (The peacock is an obvious example.) In humans, women have more different ways that they can strut, and in most countries, women enhance their appearance more than men with jewelry, makeup, and colorful clothing.

Why is this? While humans, like other animals, value attention-getting displays in courtship, research shows that men are more stimulated by visual imagery than women, and this applies especially to sexual interest and arousal. That is, a woman must get a man's attention visually. What is more, research by Robert Raines, Sarah Hechtman, and Robert

Rosenthal in the *Journal of Nonverbal Behavior* (Winter 1990) shows that men judge the attractiveness of a woman by taking in her whole body and face, whereas women are primarily attracted to a man's face. So the strut becomes especially important for women in attracting men.

However, women must also hold something back to entice the male. Signals such as a knowing (closed-mouth) smile help create an aura of mystery. Research shows that delaying the acquisition of a reward stimulates the production of dopamine, the pleasure chemical in the brain, whereas early acquisition of the goal reduces pleasurable responses (see Helen Fisher, *Why We Love*, 2004). Thus, women who "play hard to get," while also getting the male's attention, are challenging to men in a positive way, as long as they don't go too far in being inaccessible.

these guys looking at me or staring at my breasts. I feel by walking this way that I'm inviting every man to make a pass at me."

"You're wrong," I told her. "As long as you keep looking straight ahead, you will not look overly approachable, unless you have already picked out a man you're interested in and he's looking at your face. Then you could glance at him briefly and keep going. The other thing is that the way you are walking isn't very sexy because your hips are hardly moving at all."

"I know. That's what I noticed most about women I watched on the street who had sexy walks. They were swaying their hips as they walked."

"That's right. The distinguishing feature of a sexy walk for a woman is the swaying of the hips. . . . No hip swaying, little sex appeal. Swaying your hips brings attention to the hips and butt. And by the way, the buttocks are a universal symbol of sexuality."

"Let's start with the easiest variation of the basic walk, which will get those hips moving. It's called the *runway walk*. Models use it when they are showing off clothes. As you walk, I want you to place one foot in front of the other as though there were an imaginary line you were following. Also, raise your chin a little higher than usual."

Sally did the walk a few times, viewing her image in the monitor.

"I almost look a little haughty," she commented.

"True. And you can emphasize that impression by looking side to side with your nose in the air to see who's looking, and adding

The Most Sincere Form of Flattery

Sex appeal is learning through imitation. So one of the best ways to enhance your appeal is to observe the behavior of women you admire whom men find sexually appealing. (It is important that you admire them, because otherwise, you won't mimic them.)

The View from Behind

German scholar Iraneous Eibl-Eibesfeldt went around the world recording on film many different body language behaviors and the responses they bring. He found that a sexual response in men to the presentation of buttocks by a woman was universal. (See Eibl-Eibesfeldt, *Ethology: The Biology of Behavior*, 1975.)

Women in various cultures have found ways of capitalizing on this principle of sexual attraction. Hip swaying is the most common method of doing this in Western culture. In a very different way, prostitutes in many cultures bend over in the presence of men to stimulate this response. Hip swaying is uncommon in traditional Arab societies, but women with large buttocks are especially attractive to Arab men—the size itself being the signal that attracts the male's attention to that region of the body.

a head toss to the mix. By the way, a good way to practice the runway walk is the old standard of placing a book on your head, like in charm school. That will keep your torso and head erect."

Sally did the walk again, incorporating these behaviors.

"I really feel like I am bringing attention to myself."

"You are. The runway walk is really a 'look at me' walk as opposed to a 'try and pick me up' walk. The purpose of the runway walk is to call attention to the entire body—hips, breasts, legs, and even the pelvis, especially if you thrust it forward slightly. It definitely communicates confidence in attractiveness. But it does something else. . . . Let's watch the tape of you walking from behind. Your hips are swaying."

"I wasn't even thinking about it."

"That's why I had you do this walk first. Some moderate hip sway occurs just as a result of putting one foot in front of the other, which also produces a slightly longer stride and brings attention to your legs. Now I want you to turn the volume up some by thrusting your pelvis forward slightly and exaggerating the hip sway as you walk. Look in the mirror as you do it, and notice that the hip begins to go out as you begin your stride."

Sally tried it, looking in the monitor. As she was walking back and forth, I pointed out how the action happens. "Notice that the hip goes out on the same side as the stride, just as you are beginning to reach out with your foot, but before your weight transfers to the front foot."

"I can see it just slightly," Sally said.

"That's because you're seeing it from the front in the monitor," I said, "but keep doing the walk."

Meanwhile, I videotaped Sally as she practiced. Then I had her stop and view the monitor.

"OK, I can see the movement more clearly when I'm walking away from the camera," Sally said. "This feels really weird."

"That's because you're not used to bringing attention to yourself. But how does it look?"

"Not nearly as exaggerated as I thought," Sally admitted.

"OK, I want you to do one last thing with this walk. You know the heels that I asked you to bring? Try the runway walk with them on. I know this will be more challenging, so I'm going to leave you alone to practice in the hall."

But I'm Too . . .

"But I'm too fat." Large hips will be an asset for the right man. Don't try to hide it, flaunt it! That will show confidence in your sexual attractiveness.

"But I'm too skinny." A lot of men are attracted to slim women. Psychologist Devendra Singh found that a waist-to-hip ratio of 70 percent is especially attractive to men (*Journal of Personality and Social Psychology*, 1993, pp. 293–307). However, especially for a woman whose hips in relation to her waist are smaller than this, the effect of hip sway is to accentuate the difference in size between the two parts of the body, since the hip protrudes significantly beyond the waist alternately on each side of the sway.

"But I'm not flexible enough to do the hip sway." Yes, you are, but you just don't know it, because your muscles are not used to doing it. It's simply a matter of practice.

After ten minutes of walking up and down the corridor, Sally was starting to look a little more natural. The walk, I reminded her, was the most difficult thing to learn. It takes most of our clients a week or two of frequent practice to incorporate a new way of walking into the way they use their bodies. Still, as Sally observed herself walking toward the monitor, she could see the extraordinary difference.

"It's definitely sexier," she commented.

"I'm glad you can see it, and it gets sexier still. Before teaching you what's next, I want you to go outside for fifteen minutes and practice the walk you just learned. It will give you confidence and desensitize you to having men look at you, which is something that you are still very uncomfortable with."

When Sally returned, she looked proud and miffed at the same time. "It is going to take me a long time to get used to this. I felt so uncomfortable that I tripped on these stupid heels three times and nearly fell flat on my face."

"And . . . ?"

"When I wasn't tripping over myself, yes, I could see through my peripheral vision that a lot of males looked my way. I just kept looking straight ahead, and you were right, no one approached. I guess it's a sort of 'look but don't touch' look."

"You're doing really well. It's just going to take a lot of practice. Now I'd like you to do a slightly different version of the parade walk. This one is not so haughty as the runway walk, and it's sexier because it involves more hip sway. This time just walk normally, without placing one foot diagonally in front of the other. You are going to feel really strange practicing this at first,

and you'll look a little strange, too, so we won't be videotaping this part. Stand next to me so that we can look funny together.

"OK. Stick out your left leg as if you are going to take a step forward, and just after the foot plants down, throw your hip to the left. Your right heel should come off the floor at the same time, like this.

"Now take a forward step with your right foot, and as it lands, throw your right hip to the right while lifting up the heel of your left foot. Remember, it's the hip with the leg that's forward that should be protruded. So it's step, hip out, and opposite heel up—or step, hip out, heel up for short. Let's do it slowly at first."

As we walked along the corridor muttering "Step, hip out, heel up, step, hip out, heel up," we both laughed. So did a few of the other therapists, who have gotten used to seeing me march around with clients learning to walk.

After a few minutes, Sally still was looking awkward and mechanical. She, like many others, also lost some of her erect posture in the process, and looked very stiff. So I suggested practicing for ten minutes more using visualization. "Imagine that you are moving through water up to your neck, almost as though you're swimming, with one continuous flowing movement. The idea is to produce a smooth, undulating movement. So think 'step, hip out, and heel up' as you push through the weight of the water. Also, starting off really slowly will help."

"I don't get it," she said, the old frustration returning.

"Just try it for ten minutes, and then come back and we'll tape it."

The Walk with the Hip Sway on the same side as the stride.

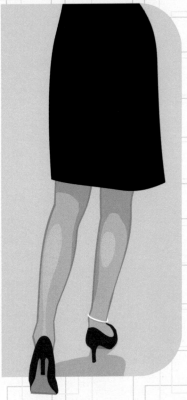

Weight on left foot, left hip out.

Weight on right foot, right hip out.

When Sally came back, the walk was looking a thousand times better.

"OK, we're going to tape it, but before we do, I want you to exaggerate the hip sway even more."

Grudgingly, Sally tried to do the walk with more hip sway.

"I have to be honest. I feel like I look like a prostitute."

"Let's look at the tape," I suggested. "Does it look as extreme as you think?"

Seven Days to Sex Appeal

"No," Sally said, surprised, admitting that she could see how this walk would look appealing to a man.

"OK, I want you to practice the walk for another five minutes by turning the volume up and down on several tries and varying the amount of hip sway each time."

When Sally came back this time, she looked much more comfortable.

"You've definitely got it! OK, now there's just one more walk I'd like to demonstrate because it's the sexiest. It's called the *greater hip sway walk*, and it's almost the exact opposite of the one you've just learned. You start with the left hip out and the right foot out in front, about to step down. As the right foot goes down and the left heel lifts, the transfer to the right hip begins but is not completed until the left foot reaches out in front."

Sally gave it a wholehearted try but like many women, she had a tough time with it. That's because only one woman out of ten in the United States walks this way naturally; it's much more common among European women.

When You're Doing This, Think About . . .

Exaggerate! It's the best way to get things into your muscle memory more quickly. Almost everyone feels that what they are doing when they learn these new skills looks absurd as they are doing it. Yet almost everyone finds that when they look at themselves, their actions are not at all extreme. If you feel like you are exaggerating, you are probably doing things correctly.

"Do I really need to learn this walk?" Sally asked.

"It's not crucial, but you should be aware of it. You could start by watching women who use this walk to get a better feel for it, and then you could practice it at home in front of a mirror. The parade and runway walks will work quite well for you, so I wouldn't worry about it. It could come in handy if you spend much time in Europe."

"OK, I'll try to keep an open mind. I realize other things we've tried seemed weird at first. For the time being, I may just skip this one."

"OK, but even so, you will have to practice your other new walks regularly for them to become more natural and automatic.

Something in the Way She Moves: The Greater Hip Sway Walk

Left hip out to the left as right foot reaches out.	Right foot down, but left hip still out to the left.	Right hip out to right as left foot reaches out.

I'd suggest that you practice the bigger sways at home and the subtler ones anywhere, including on the street or even at work. Remember, you now have the power to decide how much allure to project while you're walking, depending on what seems appropriate to the situation."

"I like the power in that," Sally smiled.

"Next session, wear some jewelry, please," I suggested.

"I will, see you then."

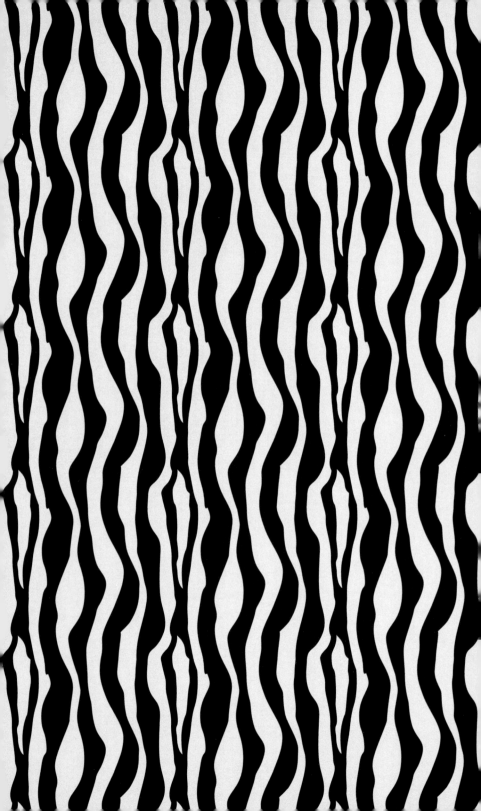

Attractive and Feminine Use of the Hands

By the time most women have finished learning the walk, they start to look truly different. Their whole stance has changed and become sexier and more confident. The changes on the outside translate into changes on the inside, including becoming more daring about trying out their newly learned behaviors.

"I have been practicing the parade walk everywhere I've gone on the street," Sally reported with a grin, "and boy, did I get a lot of reaction."

"Such as?"

"Most of the men smiled at me, and one woman scowled. But the interesting reaction was mine. On my way here today, I passed by some men and actually got a couple of whistles, and when I turned to cross the street at one corner, I caught one guy checking me out. I think I overdid it a bit, but rather than freaking out like I would have before, it felt good to be daring."

"That's fine—sometimes it's good to exaggerate a bit to make sure you own the new behavior."

Sally said, "Anyway, I'm psyched. So what's up for today?"

"Today we are going to work on how to use your hands to bring attention to yourself in a very positive way. Hands are important in sex appeal because they are closely associated with touch and sensuality and therefore interest in sex. There are more nerve endings in the hands than any other part of the skin. In this session, we will focus on the ways you can use touch on yourself and even in handling objects, as well as exploring how to gesture to create an image of sensuality. Let's talk first about the care of the hands, which is an issue because the hands get so much attention and should be as appealing as possible. What do you think of your hands?"

"They are a little dry and in need of a manicure. Also my nails are short, but that's mostly out of choice because I play the piano."

"At the very least, it is important to use lotion regularly

and get a manicure," I told her. "Long nails tend to gain interest from men, although they should not be too long, just protruding a little beyond the tips of the fingers. That should not interfere with your playing. You can also use fake nails if you don't want to deal with longer nails all the time. Colored nails are good for attracting attention and looking sexy—red if lipstick is red, or another shade if the lipstick is different in color. Black is definitely out for nails and lipstick."

"What about the super-long nails that I see on some women?" Sally asked.

"Super-long nails, especially if they're real and painted red, make the woman look like a courtesan, a kept woman. After all, she isn't going to be doing any dishes, is she?"

We both laughed.

"It's not enough to have pretty hands, though. It is also important that you use those pretty hands in an alluring way. Let's look at how you use your hands in the first session we videotaped so that we get a baseline."

Sally groaned. "I'm not at all confident about how I use my hands. I had an aunt who told me repeatedly when I was a teenager that I didn't look ladylike when I used my hands. I never knew exactly what she meant, but I did everything I could not to use my hands much."

"She probably meant that when you use your hands you touch yourself nervously or that you gesture in a gender-neutral or even masculine way. It is true that keeping your hands still is better than moving them nervously. But there are ways of using your hands, just like there are ways of sitting, standing, and

How to Dress Your Hands to Look Sexy

Clothing can positively emphasize feminine gender signals, and when used correctly, jewelry can also emphasize the curves and sensuality of the hands.

In order to emphasize the length of the fingers, rings should be round or oval. Large costume jewelry rings, particularly if they are rectangular, make the fingers look wider and pudgy.

Less is more. Wear no more than one ring on each hand. Wearing too many rings brings attention to the rings and distracts from the curves of the fingers.

A man who is interested in you will look at the third finger of the left hand. So any ring you wear on that finger should not resemble an engagement ring or wedding band. If you really want to look available, it's best not to have a ring on that finger at all.

Rings should coordinate with necklace and earrings so that the eye of the beholder is led in a circle around the woman's upper body; in addition, this suggests good taste.

Very expensive or flashy-looking rings can suggest that you are too into show and money, so unless this is the impression you want to give, don't wear them.

Bracelets should enhance the curve of the wrist and should be delicate, loose, and flexible.

walking, that are extremely feminine. After watching the tape, we'll see how you look and then decide what to work on."

I played the tape for a minute and then stopped. "So what do you think?"

"I'm scratching and even pulling at myself at times. It makes me look nervous, and it's very distracting."

"That's a good observation, and you're right, it is distracting. The way you are using your hands is not at all sensual or feminine."

"So what exactly does more feminine use of the hands look like?"

"Rather than scratching or pulling, the key to making your hands look sensual and alluring when you touch yourself is to use the tips of your fingers."

I demonstrated the touch on the neck and inner arms. "You see how the tips of the fingers are moved slowly, just barely touching body parts? You can do this on your neck, collarbone, thigh, or hip. You can even use this kind of touch on your calf if you're sitting forward."

"It looks almost like you're caressing yourself," Sally said.

"That's exactly right, and it looks a lot sexier than scratching! Now you try."

Sally stroked her arm with the tips of her fingers rather quickly.

"Slow down and don't look at yourself as you do it. The idea is to look dreamy and sexy."

"I wouldn't do this at work, would I?" Sally asked.

"No, you wouldn't, but you would touch yourself like this if you wanted to send the message that you would like to be touched. OK, now using the same principles of using the tips of your fingers, I want you to move your hair behind your ear."

Sally pushed her hair behind her ear with her fingertips with the back of her hand toward me.

"That's fine in general, but it would look even sexier if your palm were forward exposing your wrist."

Let him know you're interested by tucking your hair behind your ear and exposing your palm.

Sally tried it this way.

"This is called a *preen*," I told her, "and we will be using it a lot when we start talking about flirting."

"What's a preen?"

"Preening involves touching yourself or your clothing in such a way as to suggest you want to look attractive. Before you actually speak to a specific male, the message is 'notice my appearance and appreciate.' When you are relating to a specific man, it says 'I want to look good for you,' and it's a compliment to the guy. You can preen with clothing or jewelry. For instance, using again only the tips of your fingers, pull down your blouse so that it shows a little more cleavage.

"That looks great. Now try imagining that you are wearing a skirt and that you have allowed it to rise a bit and now are pulling it down again."

"That's quite a provocative tease," Sally said.

"It sure is. It's a brief glimpse for the man of what could be in store. This definitely enhances the quality of mystery. You can leave the knee and part of the thigh exposed for a few seconds before adjusting the skirt, or if you're attracting attention from a man you're not interested in, you can quickly readjust the skirt downward."

Sally rehearsed pulling her imaginary skirt up and down in the monitor.

"Jewelry is another thing you can touch as a preen. For example, try touching your necklace in a sensual way, again just using the tips of your fingers."

Sally slowly stroked her silver locket between her fingers.

What Does It Mean When People Touch Themselves?

Often when we touch ourselves, we are fully conscious of what we are doing. For example, when we groom ourselves by brushing our teeth, combing our hair, or putting on makeup, we are aware of how we are touching ourselves and why.

However, we do another kind of self-touching that we usually don't consciously realize we are doing. These touches are fragmented versions of larger touches, and since they are not done consciously, they are tip-offs about what we are feeling but not necessarily wanting to show. Preening is one of these unconscious touches. It is actually a miniaturized version of the full behavior of grooming oneself. It's as though we unconsciously want to check to see if we look good.

The way these habitual behaviors work was discovered by psychologists and nonverbal experts Paul Ekman and Wallace Friesen. They called these behaviors "adaptors," meaning that their function is to help the person to adapt to some emotion-arousing experience (*Semiotica*, 1969).

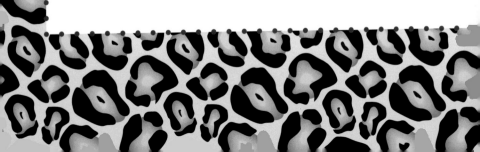

Because the emotions behind adaptors are not expressed openly, most of them mask negative feelings. For example, scratching oneself is unattractive because it is often associated with hostility (except when the person just has an itch). That is, maybe the hidden impulse is to actually scratch a person who is annoying you!

However, some self-touching is definitely associated with positive feelings, and self-caressing is a good example. In this case, the full behavior might be for someone else to touch you! And while women sometimes are unaware of doing this, because Sally has had this lesson on use of the hands, she could do it purposefully as a signal. Not only that, but self-caressing will also make her *feel* more sensual.

"The touch looks alluring, and it also draws attention to my neck," she said.

"That's right. Likewise, touching your earring should call attention on an ear, and adjusting a barrette focuses attention to your hair. However, remember that fondling jewelry must always be done slowly and sensually and with the fingertips for it to create the desired impression."

I then gave Sally a few minutes to practice the self-caress on her arms and hair, as well as using her clothing and jewelry. As she watched admiringly in the monitor, I gathered a few objects for the next piece of our session—sunglasses, a cup, a wineglass, and a cigarette.

"OK, the next thing we will explore about how to use your hands is how you handle objects. The way you touch objects in your environment can emphasize femininity and at the same time convey messages about your sensuality and your interest in touch in general."

"Give me an example," Sally said.

"Feminine qualities are shown when a woman uses props of just about any kind by the way she handles them. For instance, try on the sunglasses I have on the table by putting them on and then taking them off."

Sally picked up the sunglasses and put them on with two hands, but with her fingers together so that her fingers as well as her thumbs wrapped around the stems of the earpieces. When Sally took the glasses off, she used just one hand, with the thumb and forefinger grasping the earpiece and lens frame, pulling the glasses off to one side.

"Let's do that again, keeping in mind that you want to use the tips of your fingers to touch. Let me demonstrate."

I demonstrated putting the glasses on, again with two hands, but touching the earpieces and the lens frame with only the thumb and forefinger on each side and having the other three fingers on each hand pointing upward as I put the glasses in place.

Using the balls of your fingers to adjust your glasses looks more sensual.

"Now you try it," I said.

"It does look more feminine," Sally agreed.

"You can also reposition the glasses when they slide forward on the nose using the same two-handed approach. Try taking your glasses off, but this time use the same grip as when putting them on."

"I see what you mean. It looks daintier, and it's also probably easier on the glasses."

"OK, let's try to apply the same principles of touching with the tips of your fingertips to a few other objects. Here is a cup. Now, I want you to imagine that you are drinking coffee in a large cup in a coffee shop. How would you do it?"

Sally grasped the cup at the handle, chuckled, and said, "Should I stick my pinky in the air like this?"

"No," I laughed, "that's a little too quaint. Instead, place both hands around the cup so that your fingers entwine at the tips."

"Hmm," Sally said. "I never thought of holding a cup that way."

"And you will never see a man holding it that way, either!" I told her. "Here's another one. Imagine that you're sitting at a table with a man and holding a glass of wine." Sally pantomimed the action. "Now stroke the glass up and down gently."

Sally performed the behavior and then screamed with laughter. "You've got to be kidding! Now that's what I would call a provocative signal!"

"Believe it or not," I told her, "if you look around at bars, you will actually see women do it, and they're probably not aware of what they're doing, but at some level, the guy gets the message."

"OK, the last thing that relates to the alluring use of the

hands is how you gesture. Let's look at the tape again and tell me what you notice about your gestures."

After a few minutes, Sally noticed a few things. "My gestures are very small and wishy-washy."

"That's right. Sometimes your hands move as though they

The Significance of Gestures

When a person gestures, the message is that the speaker's brain is engaged, and the image is one of intelligence and confidence. Of course, you should not gesture constantly, but the selective use of gestures gets attention, communicates that you are not afraid to be seen, and thus exudes the quality of confidence in attractiveness.

Recent breakthroughs in research show that gestures do more than simply dramatize and emphasize what the person is saying. *Gesturing actually helps people think.* For example, if you restrain people from gesturing when they talk, they will be less fluent, sometimes having trouble finding the right word to express an idea. Even people who are blind from birth still gesture when they talk! Sometimes people will actually use a gesture before they phrase the idea in words, almost as though they are trying to "grasp" what they want to say. (Source: Susan Goldin-Meadow, *Hearing Gesture: How Our Hands Help Us Think*, 2003.)

were about to gesture but the action isn't completed. What else do you notice?"

"I guess my gestures look kind of stiff."

"Right, that's because your fingers are pressed tightly together and your wrist is straight, not flexible or sensual-looking at all. When it comes to making gestures look appealing, there are a few things to keep in mind. When you gesture, you should bend your wrist and flex your elbow, as well as keep your fingers slightly apart and bent. In essence, you want to emphasize the curves of your hand, arm, and fingers."

"Similar to the way a sexy walk emphasizes the curves of a woman's body," Sally said.

"Exactly. In addition, feminine gestures tend to move in the front of the body. Men are more inclined to gesture laterally, out to the side of the body—it expands the personal bubble they are occupying and goes with masculine stance—feet spread apart and arms out somewhat from the body. Feminine gestures are frontal, a natural part of keeping the arms in close to the body, but they can be large. Finally, you want to gesture with one hand at a time, unlike men who make more two-handed gestures. It goes with the asymmetrical quality of the way women sit, stand, and walk."

"Let me make sure I understand," Sally said. "When I gesture, I want to try and emphasize the curves of my wrist, elbow, and fingers, keep my gestures in front of my body, and generally gesture with one hand."

"That's right. Let's play copycat. Watch everything I do, and then imitate the series of actions, just as a pantomime—no words—so that you can get a feel for it."

Gestures That Really Draw Him In

In her research, Monica Moore found that if a woman is talking to a man and makes a circular gesture, pulling her hands toward her torso, it means that she wants the man to be drawn in.

If she uses the arm flexion gesture, making a circle with her hand and bent elbow that goes in toward her torso at the height of the circle, when she is exchanging eye contact with a man at a distance, the message is "Look at me and come here!"

If she emphasizes a point she's excited about by raising her arms high, even above her head, and she's talking to a man, he will often move in closer just after such a gesture. (Source: *Ethology and Sociobiology*, 1985.)

I then showed Sally the basic feminine gesture sequence, turning my hands forward with palm up, one at a time, while exposing the wrist and splaying the fingers. I then made an imaginary stop signal with one hand at a time. Finally, I used my curved hand with splayed fingers to touch myself, first on the chest as if to say "Who me?" and then on the face as if to say "Oh my goodness!"

Sally followed me and practiced gesturing without words. First she tried the arm and wrist flexion a number of times just to get the feel of it. I needed to remind her to keep the gestures out in front of her body and make them larger. Otherwise, what she was doing looked really attractive.

"Great. Now every other gesture is a variation on the theme of bending your wrist and elbow and keeping your fingers splayed. Based on these guidelines, let's see what would be a feminine way of waving hello or goodbye. Pretend you are waving to me from across the room. How would you do it?"

Sally waved her hand, palm forward, from side to side.

"That wave is fine, but it's not particularly feminine because it goes side to side, more the way men do it. Try bending your wrist forward, and rather than keeping your fingers stationary, flutter them so that they are waving up and down in rapid succession."

"That definitely looks approachable and maybe a little vulnerable, but I wouldn't wave like that to someone at work," Sally said. "It looks too flighty."

"It looks delicate, for sure. Some women even do a version of this where they flutter only two or three fingers. And yes, you're right. You would not want to use this at work where you want to be taken more seriously."

"Speaking of work," Sally said, "I have been told that my handshake is not very convincing."

"Let's see it. Extend your hand for a shake."

Sally presented her hand with the palm sideways. As we shook hands, our palms were touching, but Sally's hand was rather limp.

"The way you're holding your hand for the shake is fine for a business situation with a man or a woman, but your hand needs to be more firm."

"How firm?"

"Enough to squeeze a plastic sponge, for example, but not crushing the hand by going beyond that degree of pressure."

Sally tried the handshake a few more times until she got the grip and pressure perfectly.

"That's great for work. But what would you do if you were introduced to a male you were interested in?"

"I'd basically do the same handshake but not quite as firm."

"That would be fine if you're not interested in the man. But if you want to emphasize your femininity, extend your hand with the palm down so that he shakes your fingers, no palm contact. And if you want to up the ante and be more flirtatious, deny eye contact by looking down or away when the contact first occurs, and then return to eye contact as the handshake continues. Let's try it with you pretending that I'm a man. Extend your fingers, then look away from me for about a second, and then look back at me and hold my gaze for two to three seconds, all the while maintaining the hand contact."

"Boy, I never thought a plain old introduction could be so flirtatious!" she said, smiling.

"It's the combination of how you use your hand and your eyes—which, by the way, we are going to work on in our next session—that makes it so powerful. OK, let's review what we've done today. The first thing to remember is that if you are going to touch yourself, use the tips of your fingers in a slow, caressing way. Scratching or pulling will make you look nervous and unconfident."

Sally practiced touching her arm and then her neck with her fingertips.

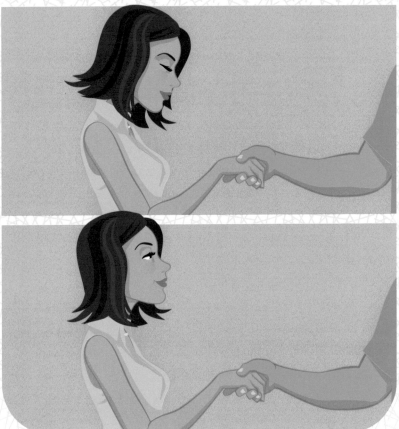

The flirtatious handshake.

Seven Days to Sex Appeal

"Good. Now, when you want to demonstrate that you are interested in looking attractive, continue using the tips of your fingers to push your hair behind your ear, or to stroke your jewelry or adjust your clothing. All of these actions are preens and communicate that you want to look nice for the person you are addressing."

Sally ran her hands through her hair and pushed it behind her ear. She played sensually with her hoop earrings and then with the silver chain around her neck.

"Looking sexy," I told her. "OK, now find an object we haven't used and pick it up in a sensual way, continuing to focus on using the fingertips."

Sally looked around, reached into her coat pocket, and pulled out a pair of kid gloves. She then surprised me by slowly and sensually pulling down the glove over each finger as she put it on. Next she unbuttoned the top button of her shirt just using her fingertips and almost caressing the button.

"You've got this down!" I said. "Finally, pretend we are talking, and gesture in a way that emphasizes the curves in your wrist, elbow, and fingers."

Sally moved her hands much as a belly dancer would, smiling as she did it.

"This is the easiest one yet," she said excitedly.

"Yes, it is. Be prepared, because tomorrow we're going to work on some powerful but tricky gender signals of the eyes."

Approachable, Alluring, and Vulnerable Eyes

Sally came in excited about what she had learned about using her hands. "I've been practicing since yesterday, and I'm really enjoying it, maybe because I can see the difference right away and it's really easy to learn."

"That's good, because today will be one of the more challenging lessons. This session today will be about the single most powerful gender signal in your repertoire—the use of the eyes. But before we start, I want to read you a quote from Euripides.

> If you are really going to kill her,
> Then my blessings go with you
> But you must do it now
> Before her looks twist the strings of your heart
> That they turn your mind; for her eyes are like armies
> And where her glances fall, these cities burn."

"Wow. Who were they talking about?" Sally asked.

"Helen of Troy. So what do you think they mean, especially when they talk about her eyes?"

"Seduction?" Sally suggested.

"That's right. Everything we've done so far—sitting, standing, walking, gesturing—is about casting for attention. Using your eyes is what reels the guy in. The eyes are about seduction."

"You can tell that just by listening to the radio," Sally said. "There are a zillion songs that talk about how eyes communicate love and lust. But what makes them so powerful?"

"Partly it's because the eyes can communicate so many different messages. But it's also true that people respond with emotion to looks from others. Even the term *eye contact* suggests this—it's like touching the other person, and you are likely to be 'touched' in the sense of having feelings aroused. There is a communication exercise where people are asked to stare into the eyes of a partner for a minute or so. It brings up strong feelings in people."

Why Are Eyes So Powerful?

Research shows that there is an innate response and attraction to the eyes, starting shortly after birth. Six- to eight-week-old infants will respond with smiles to a silhouette of a head with dots placed where eyes would be—the more eye-dots, the more smiling, an automatic response. And it gets the baby attention—people want to hold her.

Other animals also respond to a gaze directed at them, especially a prolonged look square in the eye. This will upset chimpanzees, for example, but it will also upset humans, especially when the person staring looks aggressive.

Reactions can be positive, too. There is evidence that looking at the eyes and face of someone you love or are attracted to, even in a photograph, can stimulate the production of dopamine, the pleasure chemical in the brain.

Research also shows that adults will respond to a direct stare, especially from a stranger, with increased heart rate and general nervous system activation. If the person staring is attractive and looks friendly, the reaction is likely to be positive.

"I've had that experience when an attractive man looks at me, even for several seconds," Sally said, "but I usually get flustered and look away."

"Well, today I am going to teach you how to change that and use your eyes to signal to your advantage."

Sally lowered her voice. "Look, I know that using your eyes effectively is an important part of the sex appeal package. But I'm not sure I can overcome my shyness or embarrassment about meeting a man's gaze, especially when I'm attracted to him."

"There are three important things you'll be learning to do with your eyes: signaling him that you're interested, showing him that you find him interesting once you are actually talking to him, and eventually, if you so decide, seducing him. Since signaling is the most difficult for most people because of the potential rejection, we'll work on it last."

Sally sighed in relief.

"So let's start with the easier stuff . . . easier because there are a lot of things you already do well with your eyes."

I then showed Sally the videotape of our conversation so far and asked her to comment on what she saw happening with her eyes.

"I keep steady eye contact," Sally noted, "and when you're talking, I nod frequently so that it looks as if I'm paying attention."

"Yes, it does. Also, you naturally look away more when talking than listening, which is what most people do when they are thinking. You also use other listening signals as well, such as tilting your ear toward me from time to time, as if to say 'I really want to hear this.' And you raised your eyebrows briefly a couple of times when I was saying something especially interesting. In a nutshell, you're a good listener, and in case you haven't noticed, men love to talk and be listened to."

"Yes, I've noticed. It builds their egos. But I've also noticed that they are not the greatest listeners. In my last relationship, I was constantly telling my boyfriend, 'Will you please look at me when I'm talking to you!' And it drives me crazy when my boss looks away when I'm talking."

"It's true," I told her, "men look much less than women, both when talking and listening. As females, we are socialized from the time we are young girls to interact more intensely than boys do, and that trend continues throughout life. Some people believe that it goes back to the fact that when a mother looks in a baby daughter's eyes, it's like seeing herself. When she looks in a baby son's eyes, she sees 'another' whom she needs to teach to become more independent so that she is less intensely wrapped up with him. So you will probably always find that women are better at listening than men, although today we'll explore ways to enrapture a guy so that you get as much of his undivided attention as possible."

"How?"

"Your listening style already looks approachable and supportive. You look interested in what I'm saying. But if you want a guy to be really plugged in, you need to look really, really interested, and in interesting ways. So we're going to ratchet it up a notch and add a few more signals, because the more you look like you're hanging on to every word, the more he's going to like it."

To Look or Not to Look . . .

Eye contact is an age-old problem in communication between the sexes:

Although both men and women look less when speaking (to get their thoughts together) and more when listening (to show that they're paying attention), women maintain more eye contact whether speaking, listening, or during silence, and there are reasons for this.

One study showed that if you place a solid screen between a man and a woman and ask them to carry on a conversation, the screen disrupts the speech fluency of the woman but not the man. Women want to see the man's reactions, and they want to see that he's really listening. They also feel that eye contact increases intimacy. Men are much less concerned about these issues.

Studies also show that lack of eye contact by women creates the impression that they are inattentive or uninterested, and it causes them to be interrupted more frequently. Neither of these effects occurs for men, who have a lower amount of eye contact. (See Burgoon, Buller, and Woodall, *Nonverbal Communication*, 1996.)

The message: If you are interested in him, keep looking, but do this in varied intriguing ways, so he cannot take his eyes off you.

I then instructed Sally to look into a mirror and to imagine talking to a man she finds attractive.

"There are four elements to looking as if you think a man is the center of the universe and that you are fascinated by what he is saying. The first is smiling at him as he speaks. A knowing, closed-mouth smile is a good choice because it looks mysterious. And to make it look convincing and not sarcastic, remember to use happy eyes."

"What's that?"

"A little crinkle at the outside edge of each eye. It doesn't require a broad, toothy smile, just a little raise of the cheek muscles."

Sally smiled into the mirror and practiced raising her cheek muscles up and down to get the effect in her eyes. "I think I would do that naturally if I were feeling happy," said Sally.

"That's true," I said. "And actually, research shows that if you hold a happy expression for a while, it stimulates the part of the brain associated with pleasure.

"Good. Now I want you to open your eyes a bit wider so that the whole iris is exposed. Incidentally, you can't do happy eyes and wide eyes at the same time. Also tilt your head to the side a little."

"Sort of like saying, 'I find what you're saying fascinating' with your eyes," said Sally, observing her reflection.

"Exactly. It's called *wide-open eyes*. It also makes you look sweet and a little vulnerable . . . almost childlike."

"So that's why they make dolls with wide-open eyes," Sally said, making the connection.

Smile with regular eyes.

Smile with happy eyes.

Seven Days to Sex Appeal

"OK," I continued, "now that you've got open-wide eyes down, I want you to flutter your eyes by blinking rapidly three or four times in succession. Imagine a butterfly fluttering its wings. Fluttering your eyes should recur in bouts with about three seconds between each repetition."

Sally shot me one of her "You've got to be kidding" looks but tried the eye flutter anyway.

"I feel like I look as if I have something in my eye," Sally said, objecting.

"Try fluttering a bit faster. Blinking occurs more slowly and not in such quick succession."

Sally tried again. "This feels beyond ridiculous," she said, the old frustration returning.

"I know it does, but you'll see when we watch the tape that not only does it not look ridiculous, it looks coquettish. And men see it as you saying that they are being amusing or that they are succeeding in ingratiating themselves to you."

"They'd better feel ingratiated after all of this work I'm doing just to make them feel secure," Sally laughed.

Sally practiced the wide-open eyes look with the flutter for a few minutes until it felt a bit more natural.

"Now there is just one other element to the basic 'You are *so* interesting' look. As you listen to your imaginary dream man, I want you to slowly tilt your head a little more, about halfway between an erect head and laying your head on your shoulder, almost as if you're oohing and aahing with your head. OK, try it."

"What you're saying is *awesome* and *amazing*," Sally said to her imaginary beau a bit sarcastically as she opened her eyes wide in

The "I find you sooo amazing" look—wide-open eyes with head tilt.

mock wonderment, fluttering them from time to time and tilting her head from side to side.

"Seriously, how do you think you look?"

"I look kind of innocent, and I look sort of as though I'm admiring the guy."

"Yes, you do. Opening your eyes wider than usual

emphasizes supportiveness. It also suggests a certain vulnerability, since it looks almost childlike and innocent, so it stimulates a man's natural tendency to want to protect you. Tilting your head a lot looks even more vulnerable, and especially tilting it from side to side suggests that you're very interested in what he's saying. And in case you didn't notice, there was a slight rise in the pitch of your voice, which adds to the girlish charm."

"Actually, I did notice," Sally said. "Is that normal?"

"Very. Actually, if you listen to how men and women in love speak to each other, both voices are higher pitched than with other people, so it's a good thing. OK, let's take a break for a few minutes. When we get back, we'll start working on how to use your eyes for seduction."

Sally fixed her hair in the bathroom. When she came back to the room, she told me that she had improvised looking attentive and interested in the mirror. She also said other behaviors like wide-open eyes, eye fluttering, and head tilting came naturally as she did the mock listening.

As I had Sally review what she had just practiced alone with me, she paused. "This feels funny doing this with a woman, but I'm not sure why."

"Which part of it seems uncomfortable?" I asked.

"I think the listening signals are OK, and even a head tilt to one side might feel OK," Sally said, pausing to think for a moment. "But the wide-open eyes, fluttering eyes, and head titling from side to side seems strange. Another woman would think 'Why are you playing little girl with me?'"

"You're right, those extra behaviors look flirtatious. But what

How to Make Up Your Eyes for Greatest Allure

The rule, despite what fashion says, is that eye makeup should be understated. Use a soft shadow to make the eyelid look more sultry. Also, plenty of mascara will emphasize fluttering and batting and other great eye moves.

Use white eyeliner on the bottom lids of your eyes. It will make your eyes look whiter and brighter.

Eye drops are great for whitening bloodshot eyes and giving the eyes some extra sheen.

Be careful with eyeliner. A bit to emphasize your eyes is fine, but too much can make the eyes look severe and make you look less approachable and vulnerable.

you can do with other women is to be animated in your listening in other ways. For example, you can raise your eyebrows at times as if to say 'I see what you mean!' You can also show more open emotional responses in the face and voice than you would with a man. Men are less emotionally responsive on the whole in conversation than women, so you want a balance in the amount of emotional expression, toned down with men, turned up with women, especially in a personal or casual conversation. And while you want to be animated without seeming to be flirtatious when you speak with a female, I can guarantee that men find flirty eyes charming."

"OK, let's move on," I continued. "After you have convinced a man that you find him fascinating, you want to begin engaging him more sexually. So let's talk about using your eyes to be more seductive. When you think about seduction, what comes to mind?"

"Mystery," Sally said.

"That's right. The key to using your eyes seductively is to be elusive—first you look, then you look away, then you look again. It's a tease, really. There are a few ways to get that effect. Let's start with a subtle one, eye batting. Before we start, I'd like to show you a brief clip from an old Alfred Hitchcock film, *North by Northwest*. It is a great seduction scene done almost exclusively with the eyes."

I showed the video clip, the scene in which Cary Grant is seated in the dining car of the train across from Eva Marie Saint. She does a number of things with her eyes—looking up at Grant with her head lowered slightly when he's standing, lowering her eyes and then looking up at him when he's seated, and batting her eyes at times. On occasion, she looks directly at him with slightly lowered lids for a second or two. Once, she comments that he has a nice face while moving her eyes from his forehead to his eyes to his lips. He is definitely drawn in.

"I get it," Sally said. "But that was the 1940s. I find it hard to believe that females do the same thing now."

"I knew you'd say that, so I've prepared a few modern clips for you to observe. Remember how I told you that gender signals haven't changed much over time? See for yourself."

Together we watched a scene from a Nicolas Cage movie, *The Family Man*, where a married neighbor woman is trying to seduce him at a Christmas party. As the hostess, she greets him and his wife at the door. The wife goes on into the party, and the would-be seducer helps Cage off with his coat and then his gloves, actions that allow her to look down at his clothing and then up into his face a number of times. She then lifts her torso upward, calling attention to her low-cut dress and cleavage, and he glances quickly downward to her breasts and then up again. She looks at his face with wide-open eyes and says, "Do you like my dress?" Later in the party, she approaches him with a tray of food held just below her breasts, looks at him with partially lidded eyes, and says, "Have a couple!" Later in the movie, she invites Cage to "drop by" on the weekend when her husband is away.

We also looked at a scene from *What Women Want* in which Helen Hunt, even in her role as an advertising executive who is Mel Gibson's boss, does flirty eyes with him when they meet at a bar for a drink. While he is complimenting her, she does head tilting from side to side several times. They are sitting side-by-side, and her body is partly turned toward him, but she looks at him out of the corners of her eyes. She looks at him with wide-open eyes as he elaborates on his compliment, and when he finally says, "You are one of the great women I've known," she suddenly moves forward and kisses him. Shortly afterward, when saying goodnight while preparing to get in a taxi, she looks down as he talks, trying to decide whether to invite him to her place, and then lifts her eyes to look full into his face.

"You'll see, when you observe yourself doing these kinds

of eye signals, that it will look more subtle than you think. And remember, some of the most powerful and beautiful women have used eye signals to capture the hearts of men, as we've just seen. Now I'd like you to imagine looking at your date in the monitor again. Close your eyes slowly—much slower than a flutter and a little slower than a blink. Keep your eyes closed for a little less than a second, and then reopen your eyes to return contact with your man."

"How many times should I bat?" she asked.

"Twice is good, but don't do more than three in a row. There should be two or three seconds between each eye closure and opening. And you can return to eye batting later if he needs a little more encouragement."

"And how exactly is this a tease?" she asked.

"It takes your eyes away from the man briefly, almost like doing the skirt hike and readjustment of the skirt, pulling it down into place again. A man will see you as being just a little aloof, so it will challenge some men in a positive way, discouraging only the timid of spirit."

As we watched the playback of the tape, Sally was surprised. "I thought it would make me look weak, but actually I look stronger for some reason."

"Batting your eyes makes you look confident in your attractiveness," I told her. "It also sends the subliminal message that you are not the needy type—that it's OK to let the man out of your sight for two seconds."

"I like giving that impression," Sally said.

"Good, because there are a few other tactics you can use to

How to signal a man from across the room: the sidelong glance.

create a similar teasing effect. One way is with what is called the *sidelong glance*. You turn your head slightly away from the man, look down, and then slowly raise the eyes, looking at him out of the corners of your eyes for a few seconds. It looks like this."

"Yes," Sally said, "I saw it in the Helen Hunt scene."

"It looks coy, as if you're saying 'Maybe I'm game, maybe I'm not,'" Sally said.

"Yes it does. . . . OK, so practice alternating between batting and the sidelong glance for a moment so that you get the timing down."

In a few minutes, Sally looked as if she had been batting her eyes her whole life.

"OK, batting your eyes and doing the sidelong glance are good teases. But fast forward and assume that things are heating up: It's clear to you that you are sexually interested in this guy and that he's interested in you. What do you think you would do with your eyes at this point?"

"I haven't the faintest idea. Am I supposed to rivet him with my eyes and invite him to come home with me? I hope not."

"Not at all," I laughed. "Now that we're warmed up, it's time to move on to even more powerful eye messages. One thing you can do to heighten these looks if things get especially heated, is to lower your lids slightly. It will give you the appearance of looking dreamy and sexy."

Sally lowered her lids slightly. "It's what you automatically do when you are getting ready to kiss, right?"

"Yes. The next tactic is called the *face caress*. You move your eyes around his face, taking in each feature for a split second—

eyes, forehead, lips, even nose or ears—perhaps returning to the feature or features you like best."

"As though I'm touching his face with my eyes?"

"Precisely. Now here's the hard part. Imagine me as a guy—OK, a short guy—and do the face caress."

Sally tried it but found it difficult to focus on individual features.

"You're too far away, nearly four feet back," I instructed. "At this point in the conversation, you should be rather close to the guy, within a foot and a half, the *intimate zone* of interpersonal distance."

Sally moved in closer and tried the face caress again. "It seems very intimate."

"It is. You would only use the face caress at the point when things are going very well in the conversation and you want to see if you can take it to the next stage."

Sally says, "I can see that. Imagining you as a guy, it almost seems as though I'm assessing his intentions."

"In a way, you are. You're expressing pleasure in looking at his face, but you're also showing that you're expecting a reaction—how interested is he?"

"What if he tries to kiss me?" Sally asked.

"It's up to you, but he's jumping the gun," I replied. "You could allow the kiss but not reciprocate, or you could go for it! And if you wanted to encourage him to kiss you, you'd spend most of your face caress looking at his mouth. Generally, however, the signal that you're ready for a kiss would be that you move your face toward his, meeting him partway. It's all a matter of how you feel at that point."

Seven Days to Sex Appeal

"But let's assume it hasn't gone that far," I continued. "The final signal that will let him know you are definitely interested in pursuing things further is lowering your head and looking up at him with *lidded eyes*. It says, literally, 'I look up to you, and I will submit to you, but I can make this look come and go at will, so let's not forget who's really in charge here.' Lauren Bacall made this signal, 'The Look,' famous in the 1940s in the Humphrey Bogart movie *To Have and Have Not*. And you'll see modern women use it, too. On *Sex and the City*, Sarah Jessica Parker uses it often when she's attracted to a man, especially 'Mr. Big.' So I'd like you to try this: Lower your head first, and then move it slightly upward, stopping in time to let the pupils be slightly lidded as you gaze up into his face. Like this," I demonstrated.

I lowered my head slightly and then looked up at Sally so that the pupils of my eyes looking up toward the ceiling and were slightly lidded. I accompanied this with a closed-mouth smile.

"I'll bet that really got Bogart!" Sally said.

"It sure did—he married her! Now you try it."

I then had Sally sit down and look up at me. I told her to concentrate on thinking about the same guy as before. Sally raised her eyes at me seductively.

"Good! Now start with the look again, and after looking up, look down and then slowly raise your head first, with your eyes following quickly, and hold my gaze."

Sally again practiced the whole sequence of bowing her head and looking up, then casting her eyes down and raising her head with her eyes a half beat behind. "I can definitely feel it now, and

Sultry eyes: Eva demonstrates "The Look."

it does seem powerful." Sally adds, "It's kind of submissive, but at the same time, I feel in control of the situation."

"That's a good insight, " I told her. "'The Look' is very seductive, and the man will tend to think that he should make a move of some kind at this point—asking you out, suggesting you go somewhere away from the crowd, maybe even touching your shoulders or raising your chin with his finger tips and kissing you. And while you won't often see 'The Look,' savvy women definitely use it. It's a potent weapon."

After getting comfortable practicing "The Look" with lidded eyes and the face caress, Sally brought up what she knew was going to be a problem for her.

"These are the things I do once it's clear a guy is interested. But what I'm going to struggle with is how to get him to come up to me in the first place. That's the hardest part for me. I get shy and usually chicken out by looking away or just not looking at all."

"Why do you think you feel so awkward about letting someone know you're interested in him?"

"I don't know. Maybe I'm afraid the guy won't respond and I'll get embarrassed and just want to run out of the room. If I did get rejected, it would be over for me for that evening."

"No matter how much sex appeal you have, you won't attract every guy—who knows, maybe *he's* shy, or his girlfriend is lurking in the background."

"I know. But I just don't know how to send signals to a guy who doesn't respond back without looking stupid."

"That's what we're going to work on, learning and practicing the behaviors so that eventually, in a real-life situation, you can see it almost as a game. It's as if you're saying to yourself, 'Here I go again, doing my thing, let's see if it works this time.'"

"OK, I'll do my best to think of it as just practice."

"Good. What are the situations you think you would most commonly find yourself in?"

"Probably at a party or a bar."

"Then let's imagine that you are at a party or a bar. The first thing you need to do is to make yourself noticeable so that you establish your presence. You can do this sitting, but it's much more effective if you stand. So I'd like you to get up and assume one of the alluring poses we worked on."

Sally stood up, took weight slightly off one foot, perched her hand on her opposite hip with her thumb in front, and flipped her hair back with a quick turn of her head.

"Great. That will definitely draw men's attention to you. Now what you want to do is to announce, with body language, that you are interested in meeting someone. You do that by scanning the room and focusing on specific people or objects very briefly."

"In other words, you're checking the scene out," Sally said.

"Exactly. So stand in your alluring position, and scan the room, checking to see if there is anyone you'd be interested in talking to by looking rapidly in different directions."

Sally posed provocatively and moved her head and eyes progressively across the room in a series of quick head movements.

"That's a good start," I told her. "But rather than shifting your head and eyes exactly together, it will look more natural and more interesting if you lead in each new direction with your eyes first and your head following immediately after in a smooth, flowing motion."

Sally tried scanning the room again, looking around at various places in the room and allowing her eyes to move just barely before her head.

"OK, let's look in the monitor." I replayed the first room scan, with Sally looking across the room in different directions but moving her head and eyes together, and then the scan in which she led with her eyes just before turning her head.

"The second one looks best," Sally said. "I somehow look more intelligent than when I'm just moving my head around."

"That's because quick eye movements signal an active brain," I told her. "Let's continue. You've gotten men to notice you, and you've checked out the room looking for a potential candidate to meet. The next step is signaling to the specific male you'd like to talk to that you're interested in *him*."

"That's where I get stuck," Sally sighed.

"Actually, it's not as difficult as you think. One of the things you'll notice when you're doing your room scan is that some men will also be looking around from time to time, even if they're talking to other guys or watching sports on television at a bar. That's a signal that they're not totally involved in what they're doing and may be open to contact."

"But how do I know if the guy I'm interested in is interested in me?"

"It's not an exact science, but you may notice, even with peripheral vision, that a certain guy has looked at you more than once. If he also straightens up, presenting his chest while looking in your direction, that's a good sign. Nonverbal expert Albert Scheflen (*Psychiatry*, 1965) called it *courtship readiness*."

"What if I'm not interested in the guy who's looking?" Sally asked.

"You just pointedly look in another direction and stop doing your room scan. But if he looks interesting, it's time to signal him that you wouldn't mind if he approached."

"So what do I do then—just stare at him until he looks back? I don't think I can do that," Sally said, sounding defensive.

"That is an option for women who are very assertive. Some women even go a step further and check out the guy's whole body top to bottom, similar to the way that men check out women's bodies."

Sally looked mortified.

"Relax," I told her. "The total body scan lasts only about a second. You start with his face, scan down across his body, and then back again, all very quickly. Step back about ten feet and try it on me."

Sally did as she was instructed but still felt uncomfortable.

"Let's save this one until you are feeling more confident. There is a much more subtle approach that is less risky. It's what researcher Monica Moore called the *darting glance*, and it is actually the number one gender signal as far as getting males to approach. What you do is look in your man's direction with your eyes looking up toward his face for about three seconds, look away, and then repeat once or twice. Imagine I'm the guy for a minute and try it."

Sally tried the darting glance but only held her gaze for about a second or so.

"You're not holding my gaze long enough. The effect is that rather than appearing to want my attention, it looks like the 'look-and-look-away' glance you would use with a stranger you didn't want to talk to. The darting glance should last about three seconds."

"Should I smile as I look?"

"You can if you want to look still more approachable, but until the guy approaches and the conversation has been going well, don't expose much teeth but instead use the subtle, confident-looking, closed-mouth smile."

"What about the eye flutter?" Sally asked.

"That's an option. But for now, just practice the darting glance, holding my gaze for three seconds and then looking back.

Sally tried again, this time holding my gaze, but after looking away never looking back.

"I guess you're not that interested in me," I said teasingly.

"I just don't understand why I have to look at the guy more than once."

"The reason you should repeat the glance several times is that otherwise it looks as if you're losing your interest, your nerve, or both. Also the repetition of the glance in bouts gives the guy time to consider his options and get up his nerve, if he's going to approach. So try it again. . . . Catch my eyes, hold my gaze for three seconds, look away, and then repeat the sequence."

Sally tried the darting glance a few times until she felt comfortable with it.

"It works for me!" I told her. "Now let's add just one more thing. Do the darting glance just as you have, but after looking back up at me the second time, I want you to smile. It ups the ante for the darting glance by transforming it into what we call the 'come-hither' look."

Sally tried the darting glance sequence with the smile. We then watched the tape.

"What do you think?" I asked.

Lure him with a darting glance and a "come-hither" look.

Seven Days to Sex Appeal

"If he doesn't get that signal, he's hopeless," Sally said, proud of herself. Then she got quiet.

"And what if after all of this he doesn't approach?" Sally asked.

"You'll never know why some men will approach and some won't. Remember, a big part of sex appeal is communicating confidence in your attractiveness, so you want to feel free to pursue whomever you are interested in regardless of whether he is interested back. If he doesn't respond, you can chill out for a while and then go back to your quick room scan and find another prospect. Remember, 'nothing ventured, nothing gained.'"

Sally automatically adopted an attractive stance, weight on one foot so that the hip on that side was protruded.

"That's good. Now let's go through the eye signals in a slightly different order—the quick room scan first standing and then sitting."

After Sally tried both, Sally noted that it makes a much stronger statement to stand when doing the room scan, and I agreed.

"Now let's do the come-hither looks with the darting glance standing and then sitting."

After Sally tried both, I asked, "What's the difference?"

"It looks more inviting doing those signals standing than sitting because it would be easier for the man to approach when I'm standing."

"That's right. Now I want you to practice the various eye behavior options, imagining that the man has approached and you're talking. Start with wide-open eyes, fluttering, batting, sidelong glance, and lidded eyes, and end with 'The Look.'"

"I don't think that standing has more impact than sitting for these signals," she said, after rehearsing while standing and sitting down. "Actually, it feels more intimate and supportive to do those behaviors sitting down."

"That's fine. If it's going well, that would be a next logical step—to sit down with the man, maybe away from other people a little ways. We'll get to that stage soon in flirting. . . . "

Sally took a deep breath.

"Relax. You still have a short reprieve. Next time, we'll be working on your mouth and voice. Then we'll be ready for flirting. For now, just keep practicing and having a good time. So before we meet again, I'd like you to review everything you've learned up to now. I'd also like you to practice doing all the different eye behaviors first in a mirror at home. Then, if you go out, possibly practice on a male friend, or even a female friend, and get some feedback on how it looks. If you're in a group where you wouldn't mind being noticed, practice the room scan—it's safe and doesn't necessarily look flirtatious. You could do a body scan on men you pass on the street, as long as it feels like a safe situation."

"I'll do this best I can," Sally said, adding her own gender signal to the mix as she winked at me.

Sexy Voice and Mouth

Have you ever been in a position where a friend of yours who is resistant to criticism needs to be told something and you seem to be the only person willing to tell her? As sex appeal coaches, my partner Stan and I are oftentimes in that position. My role is to help people improve, but first they need to be shown in as forthright but unhurtful a way as possible what their flaws are. Sally had many, but most of what we had worked on so far was fairly easy to change. Today was going to be different. Her voice, which did not have a particularly pleasant timbre, was one of the things that was going to be under scrutiny. I was not looking forward to confronting her with this reality.

After our preliminary greetings, I announced, "Today we're going to work on using your mouth and later your voice to be sexy." Starting with the mouth meant following the path of least resistance, which is almost always, in my experience, the way to go.

"Why just the mouth—why not facial expressions in general?"

"We'll be talking some about facial expressions, and we've already talked about use of the eyes and also other behaviors involving the head and face region like hair preening, head toss, and head tilt. Today we want to focus on the part played by the mouth itself, because it can be extremely effective in sex appeal. Can you figure out why?"

"I guess it's because we use our mouths to smile."

"In part. Smiling is essential to communicating approach-ability and supportiveness. Can you think of any other way the mouth and lips can be especially sexy?"

"You mean kissing?"

"Exactly. It's not that you have to kiss to be sexy—at least, not at first—but rather it's the suggestion of that hoped-for kiss that pulls guys in. So while the smile communicates approachability and confidence in attractiveness, it's also true that the mouth is used to express interest in sex."

"Yeah, in ways guys think about all the time." Sally laughed.

"It's true. Don't underestimate the power of the simple smile. Research shows that smiling is the most frequent behavior used to get a man to approach and is crucial to keeping him there once he

Implications of Women's Smiles

Research shows that women smile more than men. For example, in one experiment, a person looked into the face of others passing by on a college campus. Women were much more likely to smile at the gazing person than men.

Why more smiling? It's not that women are necessarily happy more of the time than men. Rather, they are *expected* to smile more, so a woman who doesn't smile much does not seem like a good prospect to a man. In fact, when women's faces are "at rest" in a more-or-less neutral position, they still generally look more positive than do most men.

There is obviously an upside and a downside to this expectation. Smiling makes a woman look approachable, but too much smiling can make her look too submissive. Women who are constantly smiling in nearly all circumstances appear too eager to please and thus are seen as having more social anxiety and less confidence. The solution is to smile a lot but selectively—smiling to encourage a man to approach, for example, but constant smiling only when involved in serious flirting in a conversation. (See Burgoon, Buller, and Woodall, *Nonverbal Communication*, 1996.)

approaches. So we're going to be spending a lot of time practicing smiling, and I want you to look in the mirror as we go along."

"I'll try," Sally said. "But I should let you know that I am quite a serious person and have been told by people that I should smile more from the time I was little. It's really annoying. It's not that I never smile, but I suppose I don't smile as much as most people."

"It's true that some people are more optimistic than others and smile more. Did you know that people can also feel more optimistic simply by forcing themselves to smile more? In some hospitals that treat serious depression, there is a device for patients that they put in their mouths that forces their faces into a perpetual smile for a period of time. You know what? Being forced to smile actually helps people feel less depressed."

"That's really interesting."

"So even though you may not be a natural smiler, smiling more can help you feel happier and smile even more."

"I'm willing to try."

"OK. There are three different kinds of smiles that expose varying amounts of teeth. The first is a closed-mouth smile. Let's start with you doing the closed-mouth smile while looking in the mirror. "

Sally lifted the corners of her mouth slightly.

"It looks fake," she said.

"That's because if you notice, one side of your mouth is higher than the other and your eyes are not smiling. So you're right, that smile can look contemptuous. Try again, but make the smile larger and make sure your eyes are happy."

Sally complied and nodded as she saw the difference. "Now it looks mysterious."

"That's the idea and why it's called the Mona Lisa or knowing smile. It looks intriguing, and it suggests confidence in your attractiveness."

"And when would I use it?'

"The closed-mouth smile is appropriate in the early stages, when you're by yourself and looking around at a party, for example. You might also use it early in a conversation while listening to a male. Let's move on to the second smile where you show your upper teeth."

Sally tried it in the mirror. "Somehow it looks phony," she said.

"That's because there's not enough crinkling of the eyes. Try raising the cheek muscles below the eyes a bit more. That will cause more crinkles at the edges and also raise the lower lids of the eyes so that they cover the lower part of the pupils somewhat."

Sally followed my instructions, again looking in the mirror. "That looks better, but it's still a little unconvincing," she said.

"That's because your face and shoulders are a bit tense. Try thinking of something that would make you happy, and try to relax your facial and shoulder muscles a bit."

Sally paused, shook the tension out of her face and shoulders, and then produced a more convincing upper-teeth smile. "I thought about seeing my little niece running to greet me—that makes me happy."

"That comes close to looking like a spontaneous expression, which will be the most convincing, but even a posed expression

Help for Less Than Great Teeth

You would love to smile openly but feel self-conscious about your crooked teeth or gummy smile. Here's what we'd advise:

If your teeth are the problem, the investment in cosmetic dentistry might pay off. It will make you feel better about yourself and may even prevent bone loss. And in case you haven't noticed, many adults are walking around with braces on their teeth these days.

If your smile is too gummy, you can modify it by just not pulling your lips back as far. Your smile will have a similar effect without the gums showing too much. Cosmetic dentistry also can be helpful in making smiles less gummy.

Until these problems are resolved, use the closed-mouth smile or mostly closed-mouth smile as often as possible.

like this one can be convincing—it comes in handy when you're having your picture taken. This smile is especially effective for signaling approachability and supportiveness. Research shows that smiling, even if it's posed a bit, when you enter a party, for example, tends to stimulate a pleasure center in the brain."

"That's really interesting," Sally said.

"One caveat: If you want a great smile, Botox is forbidden."

Why Smiles Make Everybody Happy

Recent studies using magnetic resonance imaging, a way of figuring out what parts of the brain are being stimulated, show that smiles have a direct impact on the brain and tend to produce dopamine, the pleasure chemical.

For example, psychologist Paul Ekman and associates found that a smile would stimulate a part of the brain associated with enjoyment or pleasure, but only when a smile included "happy eyes," a raising of the cheek muscles producing crinkles at the corners of the eyes. (See *Journal of Personality and Social Psychology*, 1990.)

Looking at a smiling person can produce similar effects in the brain. Research by neurologist J. O'Doherty and his colleagues has shown that a part of the brain that responds to rewarding experiences is stimulated when looking at the image of an attractive face. This effect is stronger if the attractive face is also depicted as smiling and looking straight out toward the perceiver. (See *Neuropsychologia*, 2003.)

At this point, Sally laughed, and a more natural and relaxed-looking smile came to her face.

"There you go!"

"And when would I use this smile?"

"The upper-teeth smile could be used when exchanging eye contact with a man. You would also use it frequently in a conversation with other women or with a man. However, the constant upper-teeth smile in a conversation, accompanied by 'happy eyes,' is used when there is some serious flirting going on, and it's likely to be used by both you and the man at that time. We'll get to that more in the next session. OK, now let's move on to the third smile. This one involves showing both the upper and lower teeth. Try it."

Sally pulled her lips back exposing her top and bottom teeth. "This looks really weird."

"It can. You really have to combine the smile with an overall happy feeling. Try using happy eyes, lift your head a little, and think about when you got some very good news and you felt joyful."

"I was really thrilled when I got the news over the phone that I had just been hired for my present job. It was a position I really wanted."

"Good. Now try and conjure up the expression."

Sally smiled broadly with her mouth open as if to say, "Oh, wow!"

"That's strange, I actually felt some of that joyful feeling again!"

"That makes sense," I told her. "You have to be actually feeling or anticipating something very pleasurable for it to work. On men,

Happy.

Happier.

Happy and Excited.

especially if it's held very long, this smile tends to look goofy, but it looks better on women—Cameron Diaz, for example. When you see children having a lot of fun in play, you will see that smile. It's the same with athletes just after an important victory, people living it up on New Year's Eve, or in pictures of people at Carnival in Rio de Janeiro. Of course, whenever you're having a great time with a guy, this smile really works because it shows you're enjoying being with him a lot. If you're feeling it, you come off as a really fun person, but it's not for all occasions. This smile communicates confidence in your attractiveness and approachability."

"Got it," Sally said.

"Let's move on. While smiling is essential, it is mostly with the mouth that you communicate interest in sex. Let's go back to the mirror. First try doing a 'pout.'"

"Are you saying that looking cranky is going to interest a guy?"

"No, a pout is not an annoyed-looking expression, but rather it looks a little girlish, since children are more likely to pout than adults. Look in the mirror, put your lips together and protrude them slightly, and then extend the lower lip a little farther than the upper. What do you notice about this expression?"

"It almost looks as though I were ready to kiss someone."

"Good observation. It also draws attention to your lips by making them look fuller."

"That's true," Sally said, giggling. "It's kind of silly, but it's cute."

"The next signal is a turned-up version of the pout. It's called a *lip pucker*. Protrude your lips a little more, but don't stick out the lower lip."

"That definitely looks like I'm going to kiss," Sally said after trying it and viewing her reflection. "But wouldn't it be stupid to use unless I actually were trying to kiss?"

"Actually, you could use this expression as you're looking around the room. It's as if you're saying, 'hmmm' with a pucker."

"Hmmm," Sally said, trying to get a feel for how this would come across. "I could see a model doing this."

"Of course, if you're talking to a man at close range and combine that with what researcher Monica Moore calls the *face to face*, pressing your face forward until your noses are about six inches apart, you definitely are inviting a kiss."

Sally moved her head forward toward the mirror and laughed, "He'd better kiss me!"

"Next we're going to turn up the volume more with lip-licking. You would ordinarily use this prior to actually exchanging glances with a specific man. Try it."

Sally self-consciously ran her tongue quickly across her upper lip.

"Do it more slowly."

Sally tried again, slowing down somewhat. "Better. Now do the same motion on your lower lip."

"I notice that also makes my mouth open up. Isn't this too blatant?" Sally said after trying.

"No. You'd be surprised, but it actually might go unnoticed unless you do it several times. And there's one more step—run the tongue all the way around the mouth."

Sally tried it. "I can't believe that ordinary women really do this!"

Pouting makes the lips look fuller and more sensual.

The pucker says, "See my kissable mouth."

"Well, again, Monica Moore's research shows they do."

"And what makes it so sexy?"

"There are a few things. Lip-licking actually makes the lips look more shiny and therefore more attractive—a sort of natural lip gloss. Lip-licking is also related unconsciously to wiping food away from the lips with your tongue, so it's associated with pleasure or wished-for pleasure. Watch men when they see a very sexy woman walk by—lip-licking is common."

"It seems pretty crude to do something that basically says, 'I think you're lip-smacking good,'" Sally said, frowning.

"Remember, it's not like you were saying out loud 'I want sex.' It's just body language, so it's still relatively subtle. Besides, it doesn't mean you're easy, just that you're confident in your attractiveness and sexuality."

"There's one more special mouth signal to go," I continued, "and it turns up the volume even a little more."

"I can't wait," Sally said with a chuckle. "What is it?"

"It consists of holding the mouth slightly open for a period of time. You did the open mouth before just briefly when you licked your lower lip, but this one you sustain longer."

"Like a 'mouth-breather'?"

"No, you don't drop your jaw. Just relax your lower lip a little and let there be a little space between your lips."

Sally looked in the mirror and experimented with ways of doing the open-mouth maneuver.

"When I do it with a relaxed mouth, it looks like I'm in a suspended state of awe," she noted. "And if I add a little tension in the lips, it looks almost like a pucker and looks even sexier."

The Power of Lipstick

Using the right cosmetics can enhance the appearance and sex appeal of the mouth.

Wear lip gloss whenever you can to make lips enticing. At the very least, use lip balm on your lips to keep them moist. Cracked lips are a turnoff.

You can use any shade of lipstick you feel comfortable with, even red. Be aware that some men do not like women to look made up, so a more neutral tone except for evenings may be a better choice.

Use lip liner as a guide to how to apply lipstick and to correct minor distortions in the shape of your lips. But do not exaggerate, as the lips will look fake and less kissable.

Apply lipstick in private as much as possible. While on a few occasions, pulling out a compact and sensuously and consciously putting on lipstick might be a turn on, there are better ways of using the mouth to suggest sexiness. For the most part, putting on lipstick is bathroom behavior.

"If you really want to turn up the volume, try it with slightly lidded eyes."

Sally did as requested. "Wow, that's really a come-on! But I'm not sure when I would use it."

"Keeping your lips parted with slightly lidded eyes should be used only if you really want to be approached. It's very sexy and definitely looks like a come-on. But some women keep their lips slightly parted almost all the time. It definitely draws attention to the mouth and looks appealing. So really, a better question in this case is when you wouldn't use it. And I'd answer that by saying that it's probably not a good idea when you are at work and trying to be taken seriously."

"So you're saying that keeping my lips slightly parted is something I should include in my general presentation?"

"To the extent that you're comfortable with it, yes. At the very least, you should use it more frequently when you are interested in interacting with males you find attractive. I'd like you to go to one of the local cafés and try out the three different smiles—closed mouth, upper teeth showing, and both upper and lower teeth showing. I'd also like you to practice some of the mouth behaviors: a slight pout, lip pucker, lip-licking if you dare, and slightly open mouth. See what response you get. Let's meet again in an hour."

"Well, that was interesting," Sally said, returning from the café. "I did the closed-mouth smiling walking down the street, and a lot of people looked at me and smiled back. I also did the upper-teeth smile when I was paying the cashier and saying 'Thank you,' and he reciprocated with a big smile of his own. So

Awestruck with open mouth and lidded eyes.

I guess it's true that when you're smiling, the whole world smiles with you."

"And the other mouth techniques?"

"I'm going to have to play around with these more because they are riskier. Every time I did the licking thing and there was a guy who caught my eye, I'd have to look away because it looked like he was going to approach. I felt funny with the pout, so I didn't do it. And the verdict isn't in on keeping my lips slightly parted. It seemed like when I was waiting to be served, a few more men were looking my way, but it may also be that I am paying more attention to the reaction from men. Also, I can't tell if it's the mouth stuff or just another addition to the whole package. I mean, I would expect to be getting more positive attention from men with my new posture, walk, and all."

"Well, you're right if you're saying that the mouth is a more subtle gender signal than walking, but don't underestimate its power."

"The good news is that unlike the walk, these behaviors are easy to do," Sally added. "They take hardly any practice at all."

I felt myself getting anxious. We were about to work on voice, and Sally's voice needed a lot of work. It's one of the parts of coaching I find most challenging—confronting an individual with a shortcoming that is difficult to change. I took a deep breath.

"This next part of the session, as you know, we are going to work on how to use your voice to exude and elevate sex appeal. Off the top of your head, can you see why it's important in sex appeal?"

"That one's easy," Sally said. "Women like Kathleen Turner have very sexy voices, and I have a girlfriend whose voice even on her answering machine is plenty sexy. But I have no idea how they do it or even whether I could have a sexier voice, I've had this voice for so long."

"It won't be easy," I admitted, "but if you practice what we'll be going over for four to five months, you will start to notice a difference. And while you may never sound like Kathleen Turner because vocal quality is partly innate, you can definitely use your voice more effectively. First we need to talk about your normal speaking voice."

"That's where I'm really in trouble," Sally said. "I don't have a very sexy voice."

It's always easier when a person identifies a problem point on their own than when I do it, and I sighed in relief at Sally's admission. "Let's listen to your voice on the video recording from the last session with the picture turned off to hear why you say that."

After listening for a little while, Sally grimaced. "It's squeaky and doesn't seem very confident," she said, looking discouraged.

"That's true. You habitually use a pitch that seems to be too high for your average tone of voice. Optimum pitch is the level of voice that people should return to as their pitch goes up and down to emphasize ideas and express emotions. The reason your voice sounds squeaky is that your usual base pitch is higher than it should be, and your voice is not very resonant."

"By *resonant*, you mean like radio or TV newscasters?" Sally asked.

"That's right—it means a rich voice, with lots of harmonics mixed in, and it comes from having relaxed vocal chords when you speak. Actually, I have noticed that when you're relaxed, like just after we have been joking or when you're feeling confident about what you're doing, the pitch drops some and the voice seems more relaxed."

"But how can I do that when I feel nervous?"

"First you need to breathe from your diaphragm. Do you remember that? We covered it in our first session."

"Yes, I worked on it for a while but then I forgot about it.

I need to get back to practicing deep breathing when I'm by myself."

"Yes, you do. You can also monitor your voice quality by using an audio recorder to see how much it's different when you practice the deep breathing. You can also just keep reminding yourself, 'Breathe.' In addition, the more you can relax your body, the more resonant your voice will be. Breathing deeply helps with this."

"It's not just when I'm tense that my pitch goes up, though. It happens when I get excited, too, and I don't want to sacrifice that."

"You don't have to do away with enthusiasm at all. The idea is to go up and down around your optimum pitch. Shifting pitch is the main way people have vocal variety and avoid a monotone."

"I get that, but how can I figure out what my optimum pitch is?"

"It's about a fourth of the way up from the lowest note you can hit to the highest. Take a minute to relax your body and breathe deeply. . . . Now start talking."

Sally tried it. "I'm surprised—it's lower than I usually speak. And it's also more resonant."

"And because it's so low compared to your upper range, most changes in pitch will be in an upward direction, although some will go down," I added. "Vocal variety is really important in communication. It helps to keep listeners' attention, and it also contributes to an image of an intelligent, friendly, and credible person."

"Are pitch changes all there is to vocal variety?"

"No, there are also changes in speed of talking, loudness, and voice quality, but pitch is the main one. Let's try something," I said, handing Sally a book of children's stories. "I'd like you to imagine that you're reading a story to your niece, the point being to use variety in your voice."

"How about 'Jack and the Beanstalk'?"

"Great. Just imagine you're tucking her into bed."

Sally began reading the story. She used a slightly lower voice for the man who sells the beans than for Jack; a higher-pitched, fast, and loud voice representing Jack's mother when she is upset that he traded the cow for beans; a moderately low voice for the giant's wife; a very low, guttural voice when the giant says 'Fee, fey, fo, fum'; and so forth. When Jack hides from the giant, she used a breathy voice, almost a whisper, to describe what was happening. When Jack escapes from the giant and then cuts down the beanstalk, she used her voice with a rising inflection and fast rate to express excitement. When Jack is home again with his mother, her voice was pleasant, a lower-pitched and slower voice than she used before.

"You see, you can do it! It's a matter of relaxing and controlling your voice."

"I tried to keep breathing from my diaphragm," Sally said, with a delighted rising inflection in her voice.

"One way you can work on this at home is to read passages from a book, the newspaper, or whatever, concentrating on having a relaxed voice and communicating in such a way as to keep a listener's attention. Recording your voice and playing it back to see your progress would be important."

Sally said, "I'll do that."

"Work on it tonight and report back to me. For the time being, the main thing is for you to avoid the squeaky voice. It comes from a baseline pitch that is too high for your optimum pitch and an unrelaxed vocal quality with little resonance. But I'm not talking about artificially lowering your voice. Whatever your optimum pitch, that's fine."

"Maybe my voice will be more appealing after practicing, but how would I make it sexier?" Sally asked.

"One option is to use a lower pitch than usual, actually just a little below optimum pitch."

"Like Kathleen Turner, or like Samantha in *Sex and the City*?"

"Or Angelina Jolie in *Tomb Raiders* or Uma Thurman in her sexy role in *The Producers*. Anyway, you've got the idea. I'm going to turn on the tape recorder. Try it."

Sally lowered her voice and said, "Now I'm going to pretend I'm Uma Thurman and speak very . . . slowly . . . and with a low, sexy voice, and not verrrrrry loud."

"That's good," I laughed, "but you couldn't use that tone all of the time or you'd get a strained voice."

"So when should I use it?"

"Maybe at a bar if it's not too noisy, or when answering the phone or leaving a message on an answering machine so that if a guy calls, the first thing he hears is a sexy voice."

"I know someone who uses that sound on her voice messaging greeting, and it is sexy." Then Sally tried it. "Helloo there, this is sexy Sally, and I am verrrry sexxxy."

We both laughed. "I don't know if I would use that one—it seems overdone and might put the guy off," Sally said.

"The way you did it, for humorous effect, was a little overdone, and it comes close to what is known as the *mellifluous* quality. It involves a lot of vocal variety and especially elongated sounds, like 'Hiiiie, how ARRRE youuuu?' That voice is appropriate only for relationships where a strong emotional connection has been established. In other relationships, it comes off as being excessively affectionate and fawning. Try the breathy voice again, like you did when you were reading the story."

Sally used the breathy voice but no elongated sounds as she said "Hi, I'm sorry I can't answer the phone right now, but if you'll leave a message, I'll call you back."

As we listened back, Sally was surprised. "It actually sounds sort of soothing. . . . Maybe I'll save it for a first or second date."

"OK, now let's discuss the last thing on the agenda today—how to use your voice in a back-and-forth conversation. Specifically, what I'm talking about now is coordinating talk with another person, and it's easier than you might think. The idea is to have a smooth, flowing conversation so that both people feel comfortable, kind of meshing of styles."

"That has been a problem for me, especially with men. Sometimes there are silences and it's awkward. Sometimes I get excited and start trying too hard, and the guy just sits back and listens. The other thing that happens is that sometimes I accidentally interrupt the guy."

"It's good you are aware of these things because you're right—silences, one-sided conversation, and interruptions are not good. Research shows that how smoothly a person is able to switch back and forth from speaking and listening is the best

Voice Qualities to Be Aware Of

Voice and diction expert Paul Heinberg (*Voice Training for Reading and Speaking Aloud*, 1964) describes some "deviant" or unattractive vocal qualities. If you consistently use one of these qualities, you might want to consult a speech therapist:

Heinberg would include breathy and husky voices in the undesirable category, although they can be sexy if used selectively.

Other unattractive vocal characteristics include "flat" voices (lacking a rich, resonant sound and having little pitch variety), "shrill" voices (loud and consistently high in pitch), and "nasal" voices (sound projected too high in the oral cavity so that it seems as though the sound is coming from the nose).

On the other hand, qualities that are considered most attractive:

- A high amount of clear articulation.
- A rich, resonant voice with lots of harmonics.
- A moderate amount of pitch variation around optimum pitch.

predictor of how others rate your overall communication skills. It's more important than any other single conversational behavior like signals that show you are listening or having something interesting to say each time you speak."

"So how do I know when to talk and when to listen?"

"In general, each person should talk about half the time. So if you're going on and on, he'll probably drop a few hints that you're getting over-winded. For example, he may start nodding faster or repeating 'uh-huh, uh-huh, uh-huh,' as if to say, 'Hurry up and finish, I want to say something.' He may actually say that."

"That's happened to me for sure, but I don't always catch the signals when I'm busy thinking about what I'm going to say."

"Well, now you know what to look for. And of course, if he's going on endlessly, you could do the same thing. Knowing when someone is done talking is a little easier. The pitch may fall at the end of a sentence. Or when a question is asked, usually you're expected to answer it. Sometimes, the person will look right at you and stop using a hand gesture."

"It's sort of like grinding to a halt, kind of dropping the ball by dropping the voice or hands," Sally said.

"That's a good image to keep in mind. Now let's go on to the ultimate in coordination of voices."

"What's that?" Sally asked.

"It's called *vocal matching*. Actually, it's one kind of what communication professor Giles calls *communication accommodation*, which means one person adjusting to the other's style in various ways, with voice, phraseology, and body language. So how do you think you match with your voice?"

Sally thought for a moment. "How fast you talk would be one way. It sounds really weird if one person is speaking quickly and the other slowly. Also, you want to match how loudly you speak. I once knew a guy, a really nice guy, but his booming voice was on another planet and he really put people off."

"You're right, but there are a few other things as well. You might also match the other person's rhythm of speech—for example, if he pauses for a second or two while thinking something out (often looking away briefly), you might adopt a similar rhythm. Another is how long each person speaks—it should even out over time, and it depends on the seriousness of the topic. Finally, you can also match the amount of vocal variety, mainly up and down pitch."

"It seems awfully complicated. I'm not sure I can think of all of those things—I'd be trying to think up things to say."

"Not when you get going in the conversation. Remember, the idea is to link what you're saying to his previous comment, and then make your own observation or simply elaborate on what he just said. Once you're into it, all you have to think about is matching the other person's style, and it will come naturally. And you can match with other women as well as with men. Let's practice. I'll start and you match me."

"What have you been doing lately?" I asked in a high-spirited voice and a rapid pace.

"Well, I've been watching other women to see what they do with gender signals," Sally responded more slowly and with less inflection.

"That's good!" I said, purposely using a rising and falling

pitch on the word *good*, and following up quickly to ask, "What have you seen?"

Sally picked up that the whole sentence was being delivered faster than her own slow statement.

"I get it." She then started talking faster and with more vocal variety. "Well actually, I've been watching women walk down the street, and believe me, most of them have hips swaying at least a little—some even with the hip going out on the side opposite the stride!"

I responded by talking about the fact that the opposite-to-stride walk is more unusual than the other one, but that you will see it, and it's especially common in Europe as compared with the United States.

"Now you're matching me in how long your statement was."

"You're catching on." We then went on talking some more, with me lowering the volume at one point as though telling a secret about sex appeal, and Sally copied the voice tone.

"So I just do the same thing with a man, right?"

"Yes, but not at first. You're actually really going to like what I'm about to tell you. When you are talking to a man, I want you to take back some power."

"How?"

"At the beginning of a conversation, I don't want you to converge toward his style, whether it's fast or slow, moderately loud or quiet or whatever. It seems submissive. It's like smiling too much right at first. In fact, if you're in a mood to talk enthusiastically, you can see if he will match you! But if he doesn't, or if he matches your enthusiasm somewhat, you can slow down a bit and come closer to his rate of speaking and vocal variety, without actually matching him completely. Actually, when there is *reciprocity* in speaking styles, each one adjusting to the other to some degree, it's ideal, and it's a good sign that things are going well. You can then gradually get in sync with him more."

"So you're saying that initially I should control the pace and he should follow. I like that. But what if I can't get him to match me?"

"He's not too smooth or else not too interested—hard to say which. But you can decide to give the guy a chance by using the NLP technique called *pacing and leading*, where you match him rather closely with your voice and maybe your physical actions as well. Let's say you're closely in sync with him, but you'd like more energy in the conversation. You gradually begin to speed up the conversation and use a bit more vocal variety to see if he will begin to match you more."

"Can you show me?"

"OK, I'm going . . . to speak . . . rather . . . lethargically," I said, speaking in a slow monotone. "Now . . . you . . . see if you . . . can match me."

"It . . . is . . . really hard . . . to . . . match . . . this," Sally responded, with the same slow pace and lack of energy.

"Now very gradually speed up," I suggested.

Sally kept talking, asking questions and reacting to what I was saying, going just a little faster and with more pitch variation. Even though this was an exercise, I responded almost naturally by putting a little more energy into my voice.

"It's cool how that works!" Sally said. "I also noticed that when we started to get in sync vocally, we also changed the energy in our gesturing and were leaning in toward each other."

"That's an astute observation. You're a good pupil! And actually, we're going to talk about mirroring and other kinds of synchronization in the next session, on flirting."

Sally gulped. "We're up to flirting?"

"Yes. You are entering the final stages of the coaching process. Tomorrow you'll be working with Stan also, so prepare yourself."

"Good Lord. . . . I have to do this with a guy?"

"It's one step closer to the real thing, so yes."

"Getting thrown to the wolves?" Sally chuckled, a little nervously.

"But only in role-playing. Stan's not really a wolf—for a guy—and he's going to be here to help us out. Don't worry, you'll get into it. Just review everything you've learned so far and remember to dress as you would dress if you were going out to meet someone."

"You'll have fun," I added.

"I'll bet," Sally said, matching my inflection and tone almost perfectly.

Male Signals and the Courtship Sequence

Sally came into our session looking a bit anxious. Stan got up to greet her, and she shyly gave him a smile.

"Stan, this is Sally. Sally, this is Stan. Stan is a body language expert and my partner in coaching. Since we're working on flirting, Stan is going to help us as a role-player and also as a coach."

Sally's body relaxed a little.

"This will probably be our longest session because everything we've done to this point led up to this one. So we'll be reviewing the gender signals you've learned as we enact an actual encounter. As you'll see shortly, flirting is really a matter of combining gender signals with coordinating preening with your partner and incorporating the elements of the courtship sequence."

"What's that?"

"It's a predictable course of interaction that tells you whether things are going the way you want them to."

"You mean, reading the guy's signals?"

"Not only reading them, but learning how to respond to get the reaction you're hoping for."

"That's where I'm most lost, so this will be really helpful."

"OK. Let's begin. I'd like to make this as realistic as possible. What would be a common scenario you would find yourself in when trying to meet someone?"

"I used to go to bars a lot, but I feel more comfortable at a party. I have a pretty big network of single friends, so there are parties pretty often."

"Good. Then we are going to role-play our flirting scenario at a party in this room. Take a minute to imagine the music, the people, how it would feel."

Sally closed her eyes for a moment. "Got it."

"Let's start at the beginning. You enter the room. Pretend there is a bar set up straight ahead at a distance from the entrance and a food table is to the left. Where and how would you stand?"

"I would probably grab something to eat at the food table

and then get a drink at the bar just to calm my nerves. It would also give me something to do."

"Show me," I told her.

Sally walked with somewhat slumped posture while gathering her imaginary food and drink and then positioned herself on the right side of the room with her back against the wall. She stood with her feet together, both hands occupied with the imaginary food and drink, and her eyes cast down. I was about to intervene when she seemed to recognize she wasn't doing something right and corrected her posture, but still while looking down.

"That's how I would actually do it, if I remembered to correct my posture."

"It's good that you remembered to correct your posture, but you're still never going to be noticed. Let's do it over again, this time doing the parade walk. And let's skip the food—having two things in your hands makes you less approachable, distracts you from looking around the room, and in case someone approaches, does not allow you to gesture."

I told Sally to go back to the entrance and do the parade walk as she selected where she would like to stand. "Remember, the parade walk should draw attention to the fact that you are here and want to be noticed."

Sally walked with her head held high down the imaginary corridor next to the bar and located herself in the same place near the wall on the right. This time, she remembered to stand more alluringly, with her weight on her right foot and her hand on her right hip, her left hand holding her drink.

"That's much better, but you're still not going to get a lot of attention over there by the wall. Move farther out toward the center of the room."

Sally repositioned herself to be more within the sight line of someone entering the room or looking in the direction of the bar.

"So far, so good," I told her. "Just for good measure, do a self-caress."

Sally paused and then lightly touched her left arm up and down with her right hand, using just the tips of her fingers.

"That's good—and now caress something else." Sally stroked the imaginary glass of wine and laughed.

"What do you think?" I asked Stan.

He nodded in approval. "She looks confident, sexy, and approachable. It's great."

"Now we're going to put Stan over here, holding a drink, to the left of the entrance, around the food table. He's going to be your target. I want you to scan the room and check out who's here and whom you might be interested in."

Sally quickly scanned the room from left to right, looked at Stan, giggled, and turned away. "That's what I would do," Sally said.

"Right, and that's what we have to change," I said. "When you scanned the room, you looked like a searchlight and not very focused. I'd like you to instead look around in several directions, notice Stan in one of those looks, continue scanning the room, and then come back to him again."

Sally attracts interest with an appealing pose, caressing her glass.

Sally scanned the room more slowly and deliberately, but when she caught Stan's eye, she giggled and turned away again.

"What do you think, Stan? If you were talking to someone, would you have noticed that Sally looked at you and giggled?"

"I might have noticed this time since her gaze returned to me."

"What signal did you receive from Sally?"

"Definitely not interested," he said.

"Why?" Sally asked, a bit surprised.

"Because you hardly looked at me."

"Maybe the girl's just shy," Sally said a bit defensively.

"That might be true," Stan said, "but guys are heavily invested in their egos. Remember, they usually are the one to do the approach, so there's a lot on the line for them. If you don't look interested, he'll think you're not interested, period."

"Is there any way the woman can do the approach?" Sally asked Stan. "After all, this is the twenty-first century."

"There are several ways. You could find some way to get closer to me; in this case, get just a bite of food from the table so as not to occupy both hands or appear that you're mostly interested in the food. Then you could just stay there looking around the room. I might look over at you and think I've discovered you!"

Sally laughed.

"Another way of approaching a guy if he's not in a conversation with someone and he glances in your direction is to look back and make some comment to him about the party," Stan continued. "Either of these strategies could work in a variety of settings. You could sit down at a counter in a bar or at a snack counter. Or you could stand just a little close behind a guy in a line at the post office. The idea is to move in closer than usual and make your presence known."

"I don't know if I could do the one where I start the conversation, but the other one about his discovering me would be easier so I don't have to talk first," Sally said.

"OK, so try it," I told her.

Sally crossed the room, doing a parade walk. Stan glanced at her briefly as she walked. She then picked up a small imaginary item of food and turned around to face the center of the room, continuing to look around. Stan was about four feet away. He turned toward her and said, "Nice party."

Sally glanced at me as if to say, "What now?"

"Just continue the conversation," I told her.

"It is a nice party," Sally responded. "I've been to John's house before, but I haven't seen you before." Then turning to me, she said, "That wasn't that hard."

"Another way that's even easier is if the man is in a group of people and you know someone in the group," Stan added. "You could then walk over, look at the person you know, be admitted to the group, and then eventually do sidelong glances at the guy to signal that you are especially interested in having a conversation with him. If he's interested, he'll find a way to approach you."

"I think I could do that," Sally said.

"This is good," I told her, "but in some situations, it may not be possible to locate yourself near the guy who interests you.

So you will need to signal him in a subtle and powerful way that you'd like him to approach. Also, there is a certain advantage to having him approach you. It's more alluring in a feminine way, and if he does approach, you can be pretty sure he's interested."

"Actually, crowded rooms, such as in a bar, can be advantageous for 'bumping into people,'" Stan said, "even though you may have to do some maneuvering to get close enough to the guy you want. Also, places where there are lots of people and few places to sit down are ideal for singles meeting singles."

"So how do I do that?" Sally asked.

"I'd like you to move back to your original position and stand in an alluring way."

Sally did as instructed, standing with her hip out, head high, and shoulders back.

"OK, now let's attract a little more attention with the number one attracting gender signal."

"What's that?"

"Doing a head toss followed by running your fingers through your hair."

"That's easy enough," Sally said. "I'll try it."

Sally ran her fingers through her hair provocatively as she flung her head back.

"That looks terrific. Now look around, and when you see Stan, summon him."

"By saying 'Hey, cute guy, come here'?"

"Well, that's the message you want to send, but I want you to do it with your eyes."

"I've got it," Sally said, and giving Stan a quick sidelong glance with a smile and then looking away.

"You have the right idea, but make it last longer, about three seconds."

Sally tried again with a longer glance.

"How was that, Stan?" I asked.

"It wasn't bad, but if I were involved in a conversation, I may not have caught it."

"What could I do then?" Sally asked.

"You could do two or three sidelong glances in a row," Stan suggested.

Sally tried the look three times in succession, pausing briefly between each one.

"That looks really great, but let's give him the double whammy. Look at him for three seconds with no smile, look down, and then look back up with a smile, again for three seconds."

Sally tried this more provocative version of summoning.

Stan smiled. "I have definitely been summoned!" he said as he started to approach Sally, in one second scanning her body up and down, from face down to feet and back up again.

"What did he just do?" I asked Sally. Stan stopped in his tracks about halfway toward Sally while she answered the question.

"He checked out my body—is that a good sign?"

"Yes, definitely, but notice it was very quick. If the look lasted several seconds, or if Stan focused primarily on one body part, like the breasts, it would be a turnoff. We've all seen men who do that, and it's creepy."

Sally nodded vigorously in agreement.

Stan finished approaching Sally.

"The fact that he followed the body scan with an approach is, of course, a very good sign," I told her. "OK, let's take it from the top and do the summons again. And Stan," I said, whispering in his ear, "I'd like you to extend your hand to see if she remembers the appropriate handshake."

Stan backed up, and Sally practiced the body scan with a look-up-look-down-look-up with a smile. Stan approached again, offering his hand.

"Hi, I'm Stan."

Sally offered her hand to Stan in a standard palm-to-palm shake.

"No, no!" I told her. "It's too businesslike. Remember how you learned to extend your hand with your palm down?"

Sally offered her hand again in the way I had taught her. "That looks and feels much more feminine and intriguing," Stan said, and Sally agreed.

"Hi, I'm Sally," she said. "So, are you having a good time at the party?"

"Try to ask questions that are open ended and require more than a yes or no answer so that you give him something to talk about," I suggested.

"So how do you know John and Mary?" Sally asked and then looked up. "I really never know what to say in these situations," she admitted.

"That's a common concern, because people often feel that they have to come up with something terribly witty or exciting,"

What Do You Say After You Say "Hi"?

If you don't have something tremendously witty to say when starting a conversation, you might as well not even bother opening your mouth, right? Wrong. People meeting for the first time cover certain mundane topics as a way to warm up, usually in a specific order.

After exchanging names, the most convenient first topic is something having to do with the immediate situation. It could be a comment about the surroundings—about the party going on, the bar where you are located, even a suggestion about which hors d'oeuvres are especially good. Frequently, there will be a reference to how the person happened to come here, such as how the person knows the host, but hopefully *not* "Do you come here often?" It could even be a comment on the other person's appearance, if it potentially tells you something about the other person. For example, if someone's T-shirt reads "Amsterdam," you might ask, "How did you like the Netherlands?"

The common second topic is something about where the person lives presently. This often leads into a discussion of where each person came from originally or where they lived before coming here.

The next logical topic has to do with what the other person "does"—that is, his or her occupation or planned occupation or professional training. This can lead into a discussion of current activities or plans.

Finally, as the conversation progresses, a discussion of personal interests and favorite activities may evolve, although this could occur as an offshoot of any of the first three topics. If the discussion is going well, each person will reciprocate in dealing with each topic.

I told her. "But actually, when you are first talking with someone, it's best to just stick with the typical small-talk stuff. Discussing something about the immediate environment is good because it's something you have in common."

"Isn't that boring, though?"

"Not really. The whole purpose of going through a series of topics is to learn something about the other person and explore possibilities for discovering common ground. Sometimes the person who seemed attractive before will not seem so interesting now, and sometimes she or he will be even more interesting. Also, while you are not necessarily talking about something of extreme significance, there is a lot being communicated with body language."

"Like what?"

"Like are you interested? Is he interested back? Is this a potential romantic encounter or just a friendly chat? Just keep talking with Stan, and you'll see what I mean."

As Sally and Stan exchanged basic information, Sally gestured a bit too much to the side, so I touched her elbow to remind her to gesture in front of her body. I also reminded her a few times to always return to a provocative pose after speaking.

Listening was a little more problematic. While Sally kept lots of eye contact, nodded, and reacted facially to what Stan was saying, she did not express romantic interest with her eyes.

"What are you getting from Sally?" I asked Stan.

"Well," he said, addressing Sally, "you look alluring, you're interesting to talk to, and you're a good listener. But I'm not really getting that you're flirting with me because you're not reeling me in with your eyes."

After reminding Sally about the different ways to use her eyes, she practiced the wide-eyes look, eye fluttering, head tilt, constant smile, and eye batting.

"This feels kind of ridiculous," she said in exasperation.

"It will make more sense once you're in a conversation, so let's go back to talking with Stan. Start with wide eyes, and then gradually move to eye fluttering and head tilt."

"This is really hard," she said after a minute. "I also keep forgetting what I was going to say."

"That's OK, just keep working at it. It's difficult at first because you have the dual task of performing the eye behaviors and also concentrating on what to say, but the more you practice it, the more natural it will become."

After flirting with her eyes in a way that seemed outrageous, Sally said, "I can't do this. I feel like I look like a combination of a Valley Girl and a hooker."

"Well, let's see how it really looks." I played back the tape. Sally was flabbergasted by what she saw.

"It looks really good," she admitted finally. "And all that eye stuff did seem to keep Stan's attention and a pretty constant smile on his face, which I guess is good."

"It's absolutely good," I told her. "Constant smiling is definitely a signal of romantic interest. Are you ready to continue?"

Sally and Stan went back to talking. As she was practicing batting her eyes, she unconsciously brushed back her hair on one side.

"Stop for a second. Do you know what you just did?"

"Pushed my hair back?"

"Right. What did we call that signal before?"

"It's a *preen*," Sally replied. "It communicates that I am interested in looking attractive."

"Yes. And in this case, it communicates that you are interested in looking attractive for this particular male. Preening is one of the major ways that people communicate romantic interest, so use it often."

Sally went back to the conversation with Stan and preened several times—twice by brushing back her hair with her palm forward, once by playing with her hair on the side of her head, and once by running her fingers through her hair.

Stan continued to smile as she was talking but did not preen back.

After a few minutes, I asked Sally, "How do you think it's going?"

"Pretty well. He's still smiling most of the time and has direct eye contact."

"True, but there's something essential missing at this point. When you preened, he didn't preen back."

Sally sighed. "Bad sign, right?"

"Yes, it's a bad sign. Preening is like a dance—when both people are interested, they do it back and forth."

"Do men preen the same as women?"

"It's a bit different. They might slick back their hair or adjust their clothing. Stan, could you please demonstrate?"

Stan showed Sally the more typical male preens—tugging

at his shirt collar, hoisting the lapels of his jacket, putting his thumbs in his waist at the belt and pulling up, and finally slicking back his hair on one side.

"It looks a little funny to brush my hair since I don't have that much hair," he said, and all three of us laughed.

"So you're saying that if he's interested, he'll preen back, and if he doesn't preen back, he's not interested?"

"That's pretty much true, although there may be a brief pause before he does it. It's about as close to a sure-fire sign of attraction as there is. The reason is that it's usually an out-of-awareness behavior for the person who does it. The preen signals that the person unconsciously would like to be attractive at that moment."

"Preening is actually a fragment of a larger grooming behavior," Stan added. "The full version of the behavior would be something the person might be doing in private in a mirror before going out, like combing or brushing hair or adjusting clothing to fit better."

"Since you're taking sex appeal lessons, of course, you might do the preen consciously sometimes to test the waters, to see if he is interested. It can also help get you in the habit of preening yourself and looking out for the return preens. For now, I'd like you and Stan to practice preening back and forth for a few minutes."

Sally brushed her hair back, and Stan reciprocated by hiking up his pants. Sally pulled down on her blouse, exposing a little more cleavage, and Stan stuck his thumb in his belt. Sally played with her earlobe, and Stan stroked his goatee at the chin.

Why Is Preening So Powerful?

Often when we touch ourselves, we are fully conscious of what we are doing. For example, when we groom ourselves by brushing our teeth, combing our hair, or putting on makeup, we are aware of how we are touching ourselves and why.

However, preening is an adaptor, a behavior that people use, without realizing it, to adapt to situations by managing their emotions. Adaptors are tip-offs about what we are feeling deep down but not necessarily wanting to show. When someone preens in a conversation, it's as though he or she is saying, "I want to look attractive to you."

So if you want to know whether someone is interested, look for how often they preen. You can also test the water by preening to see whether he will preen back.

"OK, let's see how it looks," I said.

Sally was impressed. "It really does look like a dance," she said. "And there's no doubt that these two people are romantically interested."

"Let's look at what else needs to happen in order for you to know he's interested. It's called the *courtship sequence*, and it goes like this: First you talk with each other, then eventually you turn toward one another, then someone initiates touch, and then you synchronize or coordinate the way you move with each other. It's easy to remember as a four-part sequence—talk, turn, touch, and synchronize. It was discovered by a biologist named Timothy Perper, who wrote *Sex Signals: The Biology of Love* in 1981, and who wanted to investigate mate selection in humans, so he made observations in singles bars."

"You mean that there is actually an order to how things go when people are interested in each other?"

"There certainly is. People think of flirtation as spontaneous and unpredictable, but it's not. It's a ritual in the same sense that all of our daily interactions have a kind of informal plan that people follow. So not only is there an order, but unless both people participate in each part of the sequence, the chances that things are going to go further are slim to none."

"In other words, if I talk and he doesn't, if I turn toward him and he doesn't turn toward me, if I touch him and he doesn't touch back, and if I synchronize my movements with his and he doesn't in return, I should move on to someone else?" Sally asked.

"That's exactly right, although you may not always be the

one who initiates each element of the sequence. Let's try it with you and Stan. You've already done the talking piece. Now I'd like you to continue by signaling with a preen and then doing the second part of the courtship sequence by turning more toward him."

Sally and Stan began talking again. Sally preened, and Stan reciprocated. After a minute or so of standing at an angle to each other about halfway between head-on and a right angle, Sally turned her body almost head-on toward Stan. Stan instinctively took a small step backward.

"I did something wrong," Sally noticed.

"You moved too close, too soon. The idea is to inch closer to him a bit at a time so that you're not quite head-on, but just at a little angle. Directly facing the other person can look confrontational. Try it again by turning more toward him but less than you just did."

Sally maneuvered her body so that it was 30 degrees closer to directly facing Stan.

"What do I do now?"

"You can wait a while to see if he's going to turn toward you, or assuming that you're interested in the guy, you can gradually move more directly facing him to see how he'll respond."

Sally chose to move just a little more directly toward Stan, and he reciprocated by turning more toward her.

"I see what you mean about how it's reciprocal. But what would I do if he didn't square off more toward me?"

"Any time one of you fails to do your part in the sequence, the conversation might go on for a while, but in effect, it's over."

"So if Stan didn't turn more directly toward me at this point, it would be time that I looked elsewhere?"

"Exactly. But since he did turn toward you, why don't you continue the conversation so we can practice the rest of the sequence? And don't forget to preen from time to time."

Going back to the conversation, Sally and Stan gradually squared off more. Stan then suggested that they sit down in nearby chairs. As Sally insinuated herself into her chair, she looked at me and asked, "His wanting to sit down is a good signal, right?"

"It's very good."

By this time, they were sitting facing each other rather directly, and Stan moved forward in his seat so that his knees were almost touching Sally's.

"This is definitely going in the right direction," Sally said, smiling.

"It sure is. What happens when you square off is that you form a private territory. And by being positioned toward one another and rather close together is a signal to others at the party not to interrupt since this is a private conversation. Now I want you to find a way to introduce the third element of the courtship sequence by touching him briefly."

"Don't guys usually touch first?"

"Actually, women typically are the ones to introduce touch, although sometimes it's the other way around."

"And I suppose if I touch him and he doesn't touch back, it's not a good sign."

"No, it isn't."

Sally talked for a while but struggled to introduce touch. Finally, she put her hand on his thigh and let it rest there.

"Let's get out of here and find the nearest motel," Stan said.

"I know, that was too intimate, but I didn't know what else to do."

"Try again," I told her.

Her next move was to sort of pat Stan on the arm during a brief silence in the conversation. We all laughed, because it was obviously a strange touch.

"Let me help you out," Stan said. "You would not ordinarily be doing a touch out of the blue. Rather, you'd do a very simple touch, like a spot touch to his arm or knee as if to say, 'Oh, that's funny!' or a touch to get attention to what you're going to say next, as if to say 'Listen to this!' Later on, when things are getting more intimate, there might be a touch that is just an expression of liking or affection, such as a caress to a hand or even to the face of the other, or maybe hand-holding, and initiated by either person. But for now, it should be a simple touch."

"Remember, you're strangers, so any touch is flirtatious," I added.

Sally turned back to Stan and touched his knee briefly as she said, "Let me tell you what happened to me on the way here." As she told her story, Stan smiled and nodded as he listened, but did not touch back.

"He's not reciprocating the touch," Sally said, turning to me.

"You're right, and that's not good if he doesn't eventually touch back. But give him a little time—right now he's just listening to you. Tell you what—touch him again, just to wake the bozo up!" Sally and Stan laughed.

Sally finished her story and touched Stan on the hand, saying, "Can you believe it?" Stan touched Sally briefly on the hand resting on her thigh, and said, "You know what? A similar thing happened to me."

I interrupted Stan as he began his story and said, "Obviously, things are going very, very well. You are both preening, and you have gotten through three out of four elements of the courtship sequence. Now we're going to work on what is called *synchronization*."

"Actually, you've already started it," I continued. "For example, he mirrored your hand touch. Let's play back some of the tape."

As we started to play back the last ten minutes of the tape, I reminded Sally that synchronization involves coordination of body parts and pace of motion. "It can even involve the loudness or softness of the voice and the speed at which you are speaking."

"So looking at the tape, what kind of coordination do you see?"

"I noticed that Stan is nodding as I talk."

"That's right," Stan said, "and I don't nod constantly, but just at certain points when you finish a clause or a sentence. Responsive listening is a type of synchronization."

"Hmm. We're pretty much leaning forward and back at the same time. And at certain points, our facial expressions are the same, almost as if he is mirroring me."

"That's all synchronization. But at this point in the conversation, if all is going well, the synchronization should increase."

At this point, Stan suggested an exercise. "Look at me and pretend you are a mirror. Copy everything I do—my body posture, what I'm doing with my hands, my facial expression, even the degree of tension or relaxation in my body."

Stan then positioned himself sitting down so that his right knee was over his left leg, his left hand was on his chin, his right hand was on his right knee, and his head was tilted slightly.

Sally copied Stan's position exactly.

"Look at the monitor," I suggested. "Do you look synchronized?"

"No, it's almost as if we are doing the opposite moves."

"That's because the idea is not to take the exact same position but rather to create a mirror image. Research by LaFrance and Ickes in the *Journal of Nonverbal Behavior* in 1981, shows it's the mirrored image that communicates identification with the other person."

"I see what you mean," Sally said as she glanced at the monitor.

"Now mirror what I am doing with my face," Stan suggested. He then expressed a look of surprise in his face, mouth open, eyes opened wide, and brows lifted so that lines appeared across his forehead.

As Sally mirrored Stan's expression, she teased, "Is this just a ploy to find out if a woman has had Botox?"

Stan continued to change his body positions and facial expressions, as Sally matched his every move. "This is fun, but it's hard," she said.

"You can practice this at home in several ways. For example,

Author Stan and Sally Role-play the Courtship Sequence

Talk.

Turn.

Touch.

Synchronize.

you could copy the body position and expression in a magazine advertisement. Or when you're watching television by yourself, you could copy the actions of an actor or a commentator. And when you're having a personal conversation with a good friend, you may notice you're mirroring in some part of your body, and you could even tell a friend you're working on synchronization so that she understands what you're doing."

"I can do that."

"Just for practice, let's do one more exercise," I told her. "I want you both to pretend to be having a conversation but without words—mouthing as though talking, gesturing, showing reactions, and so forth. This time, you don't have to mirror every aspect of the other person's body language, but mirror some. For example, you might be copying upper body positions but not the lower body. The most important thing to keep in mind in this part of the exercise is to match some expressions but not all while especially keeping pace with his speed of movement. Try to get into a rhythm with him."

At first, Stan gestured and moved very slowly. As he talked, Sally nodded slowly from time to time, and she copied one look of concern on his face. When she mimed taking her turn in the conversation, she also gestured very slowly.

"Great. Now speed it up, and I'll have Stan match you."

Sally gradually started moving, gesturing, and changing facial expressions more rapidly, and Stan picked up on her pace.

"This is powerful stuff," Sally said. "I really feel as if he's in sync with me."

"What you just did is called *pacing and leading*. We did this with voices in the last session. This adds to it by focusing on visual body language. You match the rhythm of the other person, and when you're synchronized, you try to lead the other person into another rhythm. Now start talking for real, but keep mirroring and pacing."

"It's a relief to talk again," Sally said, and Stan matched her by responding, "Yeah, that's for sure," while also matching her enthusiasm in her facial expression and her rapid rate of speech.

As they continued to talk, Sally and Stan got more and more in sync. And when I suggested that they pick up an imaginary drink and take a sip, Sally and Stan did it almost in perfect unison.

"You've got it!" I said excitedly. "Everybody matches the other person to some degree whenever you're in conversation, like nodding as the other person talks, but if the flirting is going really well, the kind of synchronization you just displayed suggests that it has definitely been a success. Maybe at that point you would exchange numbers, move to a quieter place in the room to talk, or leave together and go to another place."

"It all seems good, but in my experience, the whole sequence is usually not completed successfully," Sally said.

"That's true," Stan said, "but that's OK. It's all a matter of exploring the possibilities with the other person and it won't always work out. Even a flirtation that doesn't go 'all the way' can be a success in that it gives you practice and allows you to exercise your options. We've been playing it here as though you're trying to entice the guy, but it could be that you'll purposely opt out at one of the stages of the sequence if you're losing interest."

The Magic of Mirroring

Recent scientific research gives us new insights into the way people identify with one another and build rapport.

Scholars at the University of Parma in Italy, led by neurologist Giacomo Rizzolatti, have discovered *mirror neurons*, cells in the brain that allow people to instantly empathize with the body language of others. For example, when one person picks up a glass to take a drink, the other experiences the action, but in the brain only. This is how we intuit what other people are feeling.

We don't usually outwardly copy the other person's behavior, since this would mean that we would be mirroring each other's body language all the time. But on certain occasions, when we are identifying with the other person, we may mirror the other person and may be so much in sync that the positions and movements are coordinated instantaneously. (The next time you are having a heart-to-heart conversation with a good friend, you might look to see if you are mirroring at least a part of the other person's body position.)

Pychiatrist and pioneer in the study of nonverbal communication Albert Scheflen was the first to report the significance of congruent body posture. When examining films of family psychotherapy sessions, he found that people who had similar body postures to another member of the group would often later express agreement or empathy with that person. (See *Psychiatry*, 1964.) Research by Janet Bavelas and colleagues of the University of British Columbia also shows how similar postures communicate identification or rapport. She found that having exactly the same position as another does not have that effect. Rather, the postures must reflect one another, as though each person were actually looking in a mirror. (See *Journal of Personality and Social Psychology*, 1986.)

Research by Marianne LaFrance of Boston College gives us still another clue into the way mirroring works. She found not only that mirroring can reflect feelings of identification, but also that rapport can increase later as a result of mirroring. That is, mirror first, and the empathy can come later. (See *Social Psychology Quarterly*, 1979.)

Finally, as further evidence of the power of mirroring, we know that people who mirror one another frequently over a long period of time can actually come to look like one another and have similar personalities. One study by Robert Zajonc showed that people who were given separate piles of male and female pictures of faces and asked to try to figure out which people were actually married were unable to do it for younger couples. But they could do a much better job of matching the older couples, who actually looked similar in the permanent lines of their facial expressions. (See *Motivation and Emotion*, 1987.)

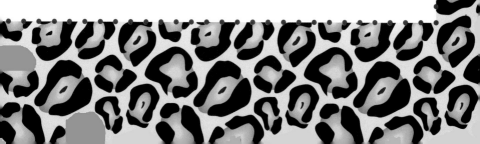

"How long does it take if it goes all the way?"

"The length is entirely variable according to the people," Stan replied. "It could take ten minutes or two hours. For example, if people have met and talked before in other circumstances, they might complete a phase like *turn* rather quickly or else just go straight to a direct body orientation. Or when a man asks a woman to dance, he may have picked up on her signals from a distance, but touch may occur right away, accelerating the speed of what happens after dancing, if they continue to keep company with one another. Just keep in mind that the sequence typically occurs in order and that usually all parts of the sequence need to occur for things to be going well."

"Just to review, let's do a speeded-up version of the whole sequence now," I said.

"First show signals that you're interested in being approached."

Sally did the room scan, self-caresses, and head toss with fingers through the hair.

"Now signal the man who interests you."

Sally looked at Stan using a darting glance, sidelong glance, and eyes up, down, and back up again with a smile.

"Now Stan approaches. What do you do?"

Sally preened, and Stan preened back. Sally turned toward Stan, and Stan turned more toward her. Sally touched Stan, and Stan reciprocated, and then Sally and Stan silently synchronized.

"Remember, it's preen, talk, turn, touch, and synchronize, and watch for his responses and decide how it's going. It's all just practice, until you connect with the right guy."

"So we're done?"

"Nope. Tomorrow we're going to work on keeping the sex appeal going and reading more signals on your first actual date. So dress like it's a real date!"

"Then, see you tomorrow!"

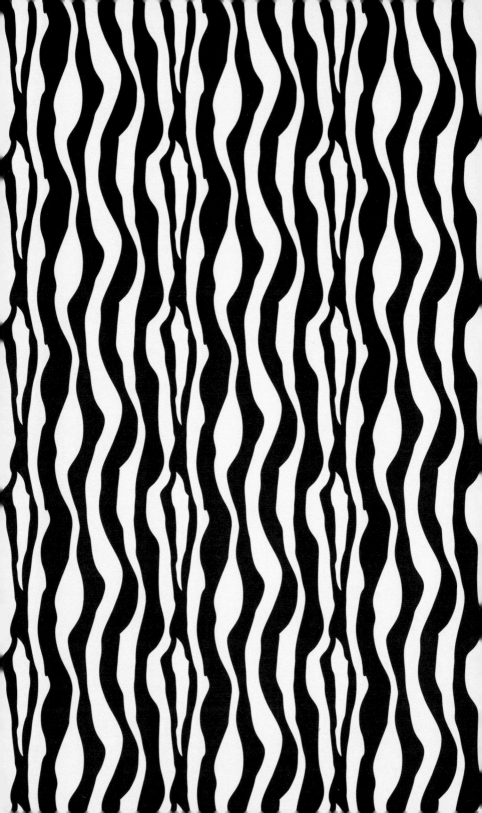

First Date

"OK, this is your final session before we throw you to the wolves," I said to Sally, smiling.

"You mean before you tell me that I should actually go out and try to pick up a guy," Sally said.

"Right. Today we are going to work on keeping the sex appeal going on the first date."

"Assuming I'll get to a first date. . . ."

"We're optimistic," I laughed. "Actually, today you will have an opportunity to review everything we've worked on—using gender signals and keeping the courtship sequence going—plus we'll add some elements that are important as you move forward in a relationship."

"Like what?"

"For one thing, we'll be working a lot more on adding increasing amounts of touch."

"That sounds like fun."

"Second, on the first date, you are going to want to make overtures that enlist a guy's help."

"The vulnerable thing," Sally said, rolling her eyes.

"Yes, the vulnerable thing, but not the helpless thing. Remember, it really boosts a guy's ego to feel like he can help you even in the slightest way."

"Eva's right," Stan said. "We guys aren't as secure as you think, so the more you make us feel big and strong, the better we like it."

"Finally, we are going to teach you how to read additional signals he is communicating, especially negative signals, so that you know how what you are doing is affecting him."

"Like when he doesn't return my preen or reciprocate parts of the courtship sequence?"

"Yes. Those things definitely tell you how things are generally going. But there are a lot of other signals you should be aware of because they can tell you that something that is occurring at any particular moment may be problematic."

"I'm not good at that to begin with. So I don't see how I will be able to pick up even more signals while keeping everything else in mind."

"It's easier than you think. Simply, any time people touch themselves other than preening and sensual stroking, it almost always means that they are experiencing something negative."

"Let me demonstrate," Stan said. He then proceeded to scratch his arm, rub his belly, pinch the skin on the top of his hand, pat his cheek, and shuffle his feet back and forth. He then scratched his leg, rubbed his cheek, wiped his finger under his nose, and wrung his hands.

"So is the message that anytime someone scratches, pinches, or rubs himself or fidgets that I'm doing something he doesn't like?"

"It may not necessarily be something you're doing. He may simply be nervous or uncomfortable because of something going on in his own head. But yes, any of these signals tell you that there is potential trouble and that you may be doing something the other person is not responding well to. So you should be on the lookout for them."

"And do all these signals mean the same thing?"

"Not exactly," Stan said. "So while I'll explain things more specifically as we go along, I don't want to overwhelm you now. Just keep the idea that self-touching that isn't preening or caressing is likely to be negative."

"OK. So let's create a date. Let's follow up on your first meeting with Stan and assume that he's asked you out. Where do you usually go on a first date?"

"Occasionally a movie, but usually out to eat."

"That's actually what most people do on first dates," I nodded. "That's because it gives people the opportunity to learn about each other and figure out if they want to keep going out. The bad news is that since the date involves eating, you will need to be especially careful with how you handle and eat your food if you want to keep the sex appeal going."

Sally nodded in acknowledgment. "There's nothing that's a bigger turnoff than watching a guy eat with his mouth open."

"Or a woman slurping her soup," Stan added.

"So let's imagine that you and Stan are going out to a restaurant. Where would you have him meet you?"

"If I didn't know him—for instance, if I met him on the Internet—I'd suggest meeting at the restaurant. But if he were a blind date or I knew him from another context, it would be fine for him to pick me up."

"It would not only be fine, but desirable. Remember, you want him to court you. So if he asks, let him pick you up. Now for the next item on the agenda . . . what to wear. Let's see how you did."

Knowing that she would be practicing going on a first date, Sally had planned for the occasion and had done well. She wore a stylish white dress with a slit on one side and contrasting black shoulder straps that emphasized her long neck and nice shoulders. She wore the same simple silver pendant and matching bracelet as in the previous session and sheer stockings with a pointy pump and heels. Her makeup was toned down and sultry.

"You look fantastic except for the things you're not wearing but will need to wear: your coat, hat, gloves, and handbag."

Sally blushed. She had forgotten to pay attention to a whole layer of her outfit. She had worn her down jacket, wool cap, and gloves, and she was carrying a large bag that held everything but the kitchen sink. These items were draped over a coat rack nearby.

"OK, let's think about next time. Keeping in mind that clothing should accentuate gender signals, what should you have worn?"

"The jacket is big, and I look like a happy polar bear in it. Also, the fabric isn't very sensual. So I guess if one of you two would like to buy me an Armani. . . ."

We laughed. "Any coat that shapes the body and is made of a nice fabric will do. And if your coat is not as stylish as you'd like, you can always throw an attractive shawl over it for added effect. Now what about the hat?"

"Whenever I wear a hat, I need to go into the ladies' room to fix my hair right away, so maybe I shouldn't wear one."

"You're probably right, unless it's absolutely frigid, and then a shawl might work better, too. Remember, it's your first date, and first impressions count."

"I think I know what to do about the gloves and the bag. The gloves should be leather so that they show off my fingers. And the bag should be small and somewhat dainty."

"You've got it. OK, so let's start the date. Imagine that you are in your house and Stan will be coming to pick you up."

Stan went outside to take his position.

"Now double-check to see that your house is neat, and then strike a provocative pose."

"For whom?"

"For you. To get yourself into the mood."

Stan knocked on the door, and Sally got up demurely. She automatically preened to double-check her appearance.

"Hi," she said with a big smile, offering her hand. "Please come in."

Stan frowned a bit. "Let me step out of role for a second. I think most guys would be discouraged by not getting a peck on the cheek if we had met before."

"I agree," I told Sally. "It also gets some physical intimacy going right away and takes you through much of the courtship sequence."

"So you go through talk, turn, and touch in seconds, right?" Sally said, remembering the sequence.

"Right."

"But what if I'm not sure about the guy and don't want to kiss him?"

"Not a good sign for him," Stan and I said unanimously. "By the way," I continued, "did you notice that he looked unhappy when you didn't kiss him?"

"Not really."

"We'll talk more about that later. You know how we said that today we are going to teach you to read other signals? Picking up when something is not going well is one of those. Let's go back to the hello, with you giving him a peck on the cheek."

Sally tried again, this time giving Stan a little kiss hello. "Please come in."

"This is a nice place," Stan said. "And you look great."

Sally blushed, looked coyly down and then up again, and grinned and preened at the same time. "Thanks," she said in a low, sensuous voice. "I'll be back in a minute, just let me get my things."

Sally came back a few minutes later with my handbag that she decided to borrow for the exercise and started putting on her coat.

"Stop!" I said.

"I'm just putting on my jacket. What could be wrong with that?"

"You are missing the first opportunity for him to help you."

"What if the man doesn't know that he's supposed to help me with my coat?"

"If it's obvious enough, he'll figure it out. Besides helping you, which makes me feel important," Stan said, "it also affords me another opportunity to touch in an appropriate way."

"I never thought of it that way."

"OK, let's go," Stan said, putting his hand ever so gently on Sally's back to guide her.

"Yet another touch opportunity?" she grinned.

"You've got it."

Since Sally lives in the city, it was agreed that she and Stan would probably walk to the restaurant or grab a cab. "I guess I should let him hail the cab, and if he did have a car, I would wait a bit before opening the car door to see if he opens it for me, right?"

"Exactly. But let's pretend for now that the restaurant isn't far and you can walk."

As Sally and Stan started parading around the maze of offices with me following, they chatted a bit about how their week went.

Doing Things for You Boosts His Ego

Signaling a man that you would like him to help you in some way, or what researcher Monica Moore (1985) calls "aid solicitation," is a common female behavior that can make a man feel needed and powerful as well as present an opportunity for touch. What are the best ways to ask for aid?

- Hand your jacket to the man, and allow him to help you put it on.
- Wait by a chair to let him pull it out for you, or hold a cigarette for lighting, or just look briefly at an empty glass, a couple times if necessary, to indicate a drink to be refilled.
- Delay doing something for yourself. For example, you could look at your coat and then smile at the man. Hopefully, he will catch on.

Stan talked about the restaurant and his hope that she would like it. At first, Stan walked too fast for Sally, and she had to catch up.

"How do you feel about Stan walking so fast?" I asked.

"Like he's not in sync with me."

"He's not. So I would suggest that you go at a comfortable pace for you and let Stan match your pace."

Sally tried it and Stan slowed down. "Yeah, I tend to walk too fast trying to get somewhere," he commented.

"And as some positive reinforcement," I added, "you might try walking closer to him to allow for an occasional body brush, which would signal to him that you are not adverse to him touching you."

When they arrived at "the restaurant," Sally did her best to pretend she was slowly and sensually unzipping her jacket. She positioned herself briefly to Stan's side but without actually starting to take off her garment so that it was easy for Stan to help her remove it. She also sensually loosened the fingers on her gloves before removing them.

I played the maître d' and the waitress. "May I help you?"

"Reservations for two. The name is Jones."

"Come right this way." I parked Stan and Sally at our mock table and showed Sally her seat with a hand gesture, backing off and letting Stan pull out the chair for her. Sally sat in her chair as if she had never done the coaching.

"Try again. . . . Remember, insinuate yourself into the chair and curve your skirt under your derriere. It's much sexier."

Sally insinuated herself into the chair, and Stan sat diagonally from her so that he could be closer, although we agreed that in

Getting Started

In Stan's book *The Right Touch: Understanding and Using the Language of Physical Contact* (1994), he notes that certain kinds of touches are the easiest and most appropriate ways to start touching in a relationship.

Touches associated with saying hello or goodbye, like patting someone on the back or a peck on the cheek, are safe and nonthreatening.

A touch as if to say "Oh, listen to this," or "That's so funny," usually to a nonvulnerable body part like the arm, shoulder, or elbow or the thigh or knee if you are both seated, will get a person's attention.

"Accidental" touches like passing by or sitting, standing, or walking close so that a brush is possible or leaning forward during conversation, even with a breast brush for the daring, are ways of sneaking in contact.

Also touches that ostensibly accomplish a task, such as brushing lint off a jacket or touching what is referred to while commenting on a person's appearance, saying something like "Your hair is so curly" or "I love your ring," are very effective ways of making physical contact.

many restaurants this would not be possible. They smiled a bit nervously at each other.

"This would be a good time to do a preen," I suggested to Sally. "It will let him know that you are here for him."

Sally tossed her hair and briefly ran her hand behind her ear. Stan responded by touching the collar of his shirt.

"May I get you something to drink?"

Stan motioned to Sally. "Red wine, please."

"I'll have the same."

"So how have you been since I've seen you last?" Stan asked.

Sally then went into a long monologue about how her boss was driving her crazy and how stressful her job was. Rather than smiling and opening her eyes wide as if she were happy to be with him, she looked down a lot and didn't smile much at all. Stan offered a few supportive, "I see's" and nods, but after a few minutes, his face had a blank look, his lips were pressed slightly together, and he was rubbing his cheek.

"Let's stop for a minute and look at what's happening. How do you think Stan is feeling about what you're saying?"

"He seems supportive," Sally said, a bit confused.

"Actually, he was supportive at first, but you lost him. Did you notice that he got out of sync with you when he stopped nodding and showing reactions to what you were saying?"

"Yes, I noticed, but I didn't know what it meant."

"He also rubbed his cheek several times."

"The negative self-touching stuff, right?"

"Right. It's not a good sign."

"What does it mean?"

"It could mean a few things," Stan said. "It could be that I'm just nervous and I'm trying to soothe myself. But more often, rubbing or patting yourself is a 'self-stimulating' behavior. It often means that the person is having trouble staying awake or involved. It's likely he's losing interest in the direction the conversation is taking."

"So what you're saying is that Stan found what I was saying boring."

"Probably," I said. "It's a good idea on a first date to be as positive as possible."

Touches That Signal Trouble

Self-stimulating touches like patting or rubbing the face suggest that the person is losing interest and trying to stay alert. (And yes, on occasion, he might not have been able to sleep well the night before.)

Self-pinching, usually done in the region of the neck, is frequently associated with guilt. (The fuller version of the behavior is to pinch oneself until it hurts.)

Self-soothing behaviors suggest that the person is feeling anxious. The most common versions are stomach touching or rubbing (anxiety is felt most in the stomach) and fingers and thumb reaching toward the mouth, somewhat like the way thumb-sucking occurs when a child is anxious.

"You mean I should lie? My week at work really was rough."

"You shouldn't lie, but you should emphasize the positive. So you might say that work was a bit stressful, but mention other things that were good. Also, you talked for a long time without asking Stan about himself."

"That's a good point," Stan said. "One of the things you want to do on a first date with a guy is show you are interested in him. The balance of talking to listening should be about equal in any two-person conversation. It's called *good turn-taking skills*, and it means that you avoid interrupting, for starters."

"OK, let's back up and start the conversation again."

This time, Sally was more upbeat, smiled and batted her eyes, and quickly turned the conversation over to Stan. "And what about your week?" she said in as close to a coo as she could muster.

"Here you are," I said, handing them their wine glasses. Sally immediately picked up the glass as she was taught, and Stan offered a toast. "To getting to know each other," he clinked.

"My week was terrific, actually," Stan said excitedly. "We got a really interesting project, and everyone is really anxious to work on it." Sally was nodding enthusiastically in sync with the tempo of Stan's words.

"What's the project on?"

"We've been asked to study what qualities make men and women charismatic."

"That's sooo interesting," Sally said, leaning in and fluttering her eyes. Then she turned to me. "Time-out. I have a question. I know what Stan does, so I know he's being truthful. But some of my friends have had bad experiences with guys who lie about what they do, or where they live, or what kind of car they drive. So how could I tell if someone I was dating were lying?"

"Good question. And your concerns are not entirely unwarranted. Research shows that while women tend to lie to protect another person's image, men are more likely to lie to build up their own image. You can tell if someone is lying if their eyes suddenly dart side to side, they cover a part of their face with their hand, or there is a sudden rise in vocal pitch. It's best not to be too suspicious, but if you see those kinds of behaviors, you may want to ask for more details."

"Got it."

"Let's get back to your date. You were just commenting on Stan's project."

"Your project sounds great!" she said, fluttering her eyes.

I came over as the waitress again. "Are you ready to order?"

Sally was about to answer when Stan interjected. "It would be a good idea to ask me what I think is good on the menu."

"Enlisting aid again," Sally nodded and then got back into role. "So Stan, what do you think is good here?"

"Everything is great. If you like spicy, I love the chicken cacciatore. If you like milder, the pasta puttanesca is great."

"I'll have the chicken like the man suggested," Sally said, smiling. Without his being aware of it, Stan's chest puffed up slightly.

"Pasta for me," Stan said.

"So," Sally continued, "have you been in a recent relationship?"

"Not for about a year. It just didn't work out." As he said this, Stan rubbed his finger under his nose.

"May I ask why not?"

Stan paused and placed his hand on the back of his head.

"Stop," I told Sally. "He gave you two signs that he didn't like the direction of the conversation. Did you see that?"

"Yes, I did, but only after the fact. It happened so fast."

"Don't worry. It will take time and practice to catch these cues as they come up. It's a good start that you noticed them, though."

"Well, I noticed the self-touching, but again, other than you saying that this was a negative sign, I didn't know what those signals meant."

"Rubbing my finger under my nose is called a *nose wipe*, and it usually suggests that something happened that a person would rather hadn't happened."

"You mean I shouldn't have asked you about your last relationship?"

"Probably not. Or when I reacted negatively, it would have been better if you had found a way to drop the subject like saying, 'I'm sorry, I didn't mean to make you feel uncomfortable.'"

"And what did it mean when I asked why the relationship ended and you touched yourself on the back of your head?"

"That's called the *defensive beating posture*, and in a nutshell, it means that you've put me on the spot," Stan said. "This is actually one of those unconscious behaviors that have their origins in early childhood experience, but the impulse remains when we're adults. The full version of the behavior would be preparing to deliver a blow, but of course, even a child can't hit without getting in trouble, so he or she learns to fake it and rub the back of the neck."

"That's fascinating," Sally said. "OK, I'll notice it after this. At the same time, I understand what you're saying, but if I really wanted to get to know a guy in this situation, his relationships would be an important issue for me. Maybe it would be better if I talked about my last relationship first."

"Why don't you try it, and we'll see what happens."

Sally began to talk about her last relationship, explaining that while there were a lot of good things in the relationship like having similar interests, her previous boyfriend was inconsiderate. Oftentimes, she said, she wouldn't hear from him for days. As she continued, Stan scratched himself on his upper chest as he listened to Sally's complaints. This time, Sally caught the negative signal.

"Uh-oh, I'm in trouble again, right?"

"Yup."

"Besides being negative, what does scratching mean?"

"Usually annoyance," Stan said. "I didn't want to hear about your past relationship. I felt I was being warned—'Don't be inconsiderate.' I also didn't want to be compared to your previous guy."

"OK, I stand corrected," Sally said, with slightly furrowed eyebrows. "I'll try to be more positive and not quite so personal."

"At least not on the first date," I told her. "It's valid to want the information you're asking for, but at a later date. No one wants to feel as if they are being interrogated so early in the game."

Sally started again, this time changing the subject and interjecting a compliment, "You seem like you're in really good shape, Stan."

"Well thanks. I play tennis several times a week, and I work out on weight equipment."

"It shows."

"You look very fit, too. You must exercise a lot, too."

"I do work out at an exercise club, mainly doing treadmill workouts. I also like biking and hiking whenever I can get out of town."

"All this is very good," I interjected. "Not only is the conversation on positive things, but it also expresses attraction when you refer to the other person's attractive physical attributes. Go ahead."

Stan continued. "I love biking and hiking, too. We should try to do those things soon."

"I'd like that a lot."

"You're making future plans, so it's obvious that things are going well now. Time to get back to the renewal of the courtship sequence. Right now you're turning your heads toward one another as you talk, but you're not squaring off. Now would be a good time to turn more toward one another."

Sally turned more directly toward Stan. After a few more verbal exchanges, he began to turn in her direction, so they were almost, but not quite, facing each other head-on.

The imaginary food arrived. Both Sally and Stan thanked me.

"Time-out again," Sally said. "Eating can be a turn-on or a turn-off. Any hints?"

The Origins of Some Negative Signals

Scratching oneself is oftentimes associated with annoyance or hostility. The fuller version of the behavior might be actually scratching the other person.

The *nose wipe* involves the person drawing a finger back and forth just under the nose, almost as if to clear away debris, and it's often a censoring signal, translatable as either "I wish you hadn't done or said what you just did" or "I wish I hadn't done or said what I just did." Its origin is probably holding one's nose as if to say "This stinks."

Rapid drumming of the fingers on a surface will often express the desire to have the other person move the conversation along more quickly.

Foot-shuffling by a person who is sitting down looks like the action the person would like to take—get those feet moving and get out of here!

"Yes. While you obviously need to tilt your head down as you spear your food, you definitely should not slump over your food, look down too much of the time, or fail to keep the conversation going. And obviously you shouldn't talk with your mouth full. If you want to turn up the volume, you could look at the guy as you insert the food in your mouth, although this would indicate that you're feeling rather sexy. Another sexy move is to offer him a bite and then place it in his mouth while looking at his mouth and then his eyes."

"I'll try the second one. . . . This is delicious," Sally said, looking at Stan. "Do you want a bite?"

"Sure."

Sally put food on a fork and presented it to Stan while looking at his mouth and then his eyes. Stan took the imaginary bite.

"I like that a lot," I said, "very sexy."

"So do you like opera?" Stan asked.

"I love opera!" Sally said, leaning forward and touching Stan on his forearm.

"Good move," I said. "We're at the touch phase of the courtship sequence."

"But how can I get him to touch back?"

"You've already leaned toward him. You could remain leaning toward him some as you talk, so you're in touch range."

Eventually, Stan reached out and touched Sally on the upper arm, ostensibly to get her attention, and said, "They are playing *Carmen* at the opera house next month. Have you ever seen it?"

"No, but I'd love to!" Sally said with a grin.

"Maybe I could get tickets."

"That would be wonderful."

"Things seem to be going really well now. Where do I go from here?" asked Sally.

"You should continue the conversation, perhaps talking about what you really like about opera, asking Stan about other things he really likes to do, expressing your love of travel, and in general, emphasizing things you have in common. This would be a good time to work on synchronizing with him since it expresses identification or empathy with the other person."

"But what if I just feel comfortable in the conversation at this point but I'm not feeling 'at one' with him?"

"It doesn't matter. Matching and mirroring can be a way of feeling more empathetic and letting the other person know you would like to be in sync with him."

"I have to remember how we did this before. OK, I think I can do it." Sally paused, and then looked at Stan. "You said before that you really love travel. . . ."

As Stan began to talk enthusiastically about a recent trip to Italy, Sally nodded, and her facial reactions at the end of each of Stan's sentences matched his heightened energy. When he gestured with one hand and shifted to the other, Sally tilted her head from one side to the other in sync with his gestures. At one point, Stan leaned forward rather close to Sally, with his left elbow resting on the table and his left hand cupping his jaw and cheek.

"Oh my gosh, I just realized I'm mirroring his posture with my right elbow and hand without even consciously trying," Sally said.

Touch Invitations

In his research, Stan (1994) has found that there are various ways people can encourage others to touch them.

Touching the other person in itself suggests that the person would like to be touched back. Also, positioning for touch, when the person stands, sits, or leans toward the other person, within the intimate range of under one-and-a-half feet, provides an invitation to touch by placing the person close enough to be touched readily.

Swaying in the other person's direction, especially at a time of departure, indicates a desire for a hug. Likewise, if one person displays a movement with both hands in the direction of the other person, it suggests a desire for a hug.

Self-touching also suggests the desire for a touch, especially self-touching in a sensual way around the neck and clavicle area by the woman. The message is, "Touch me, you fool!" A sensitive man could respond by touching her someplace, perhaps on her face, as he makes a compliment about her appearance or expresses enjoyment of her company.

"Good work. You're also pretty close now, within what is called the intimate, foot-and-a-half zone."

"Does this mean we're getting ready to kiss?"

"It could be—it's up to you."

"OK, let's suppose I did want a guy to kiss me. What would I do to make sure he gets the hint?"

"You could preen some more. You haven't done much preening lately." Sally complied, and Stan preened back.

"Now try a face-caress with your eyes," I continued. "Cast your eyes around his face, pausing briefly on each feature, but come home with each round of face-caressing to look at his mouth." Sally did this while continuing to talk.

Stan smiled. "I have to say that behavior is pretty enticing."

"Now push your face slightly forward toward his," I recommended.

Stan's lips came toward Sally's, stopping short of an actual kiss so as not to go too far in the role-playing, and then Stan sat back, and we all laughed.

"That works," Stan said.

"OK, let's fast-forward and say that the dinner and conversation are winding down. The check has come. Take it from there."

"Should I let him pay?"

"Generally yes, on the first date. If you meet up with a guy who says he wants to 'hang out' with you and he pays, it's a date. If you want, you can offer to pay, but phrase it like 'Would you like to split it?' He should get the hint. Let the guy display his resources and generosity. Maybe you can pay at a later time."

Sally practices mirroring and kissable lips with author Stan.

As Stan and Sally prepared to leave the restaurant, Sally paused before putting on her jacket, giving Stan a chance to help her put in on, and he responded. Sally and Stan walked through the corridors of the office as if going to her place. "Should I hold his hand?" Sally asked.

"Walk close by him and let him initiate hand-holding or putting his arm around you, and you can reciprocate."

Arriving at Sally's "door," they said goodnight, and Stan said, "I'll call you soon." But then, almost simultaneously, he rubbed his finger under his nose.

"Oh, boy. I thought it was going well, but that signal was negative. . . . His mouth was saying one thing, but his body language was saying another."

To Kiss or Not to Kiss

Monica Moore's research revealed several methods women use to get men to kiss them.

Whispering in the man's ear brings the woman's face very close to his, and if she doesn't pull back far from that position, it's easy for him to press lips to lips.

The "face-to-face" move involves the woman pressing her face forward within a few inches of the man's face.

Puckered lips are another sure sign that she is ready for a kiss.

If, on the other hand, it looks as though the guy is going to attempt a kiss and you're not wanting it or ready for it, you can pull back a bit—let's say to the outer edge of the foot-and-a-half intimate zone or farther—without being too obvious about withdrawing.

And of course, another opportunity for a kiss will be at your door. If you'd like to be kissed, fumble a bit with your keys.

"And when this happens, almost always the body language message should prevail," I told her.

Stan started to laugh. "That was just a trick to see if you were watching," he confessed. "It would be unlikely if the date went as we rehearsed it that I would not want to see you. I was just testing to see if you were watching."

"Funny," said Sally. "Just what I need, more confusion."

"Sorry," Stan said. "Actually, if this were real life, I would think that we had a successful first date, and if we had kissed earlier, we would kiss again here."

"I agree! It was a successful first date," I chimed in. "I think you are ready to graduate and try out what you have been learning for real."

Epilogue

Sex Appeal
in the Workplace

We generally recommend after initial coaching that the client take some time to review the tapes and practice the new behaviors before returning for the final session. It takes time for even the best of students to begin developing muscle memory—that indefinable and undeniable point when a person stops thinking about what she is doing and just starts doing it spontaneously. It is unfortunate but understandable that most of our clients are intent on confidentiality and therefore are not open to our showing their tapes to others. However, in our seminars, we typically have the audience applauding at the changes someone can make in two hours. So imagine the dramatic difference after seven sessions!

Sally had been a good student. She spent time practicing everything she had learned, and the payoff was great. She had been asked on a lot of dates, felt really good about herself, and noticed that people seemed to be responding to her better at play and at work. We could see why. Truly, Sally looked like a different person: more attractive, more confident, and definitely sexier.

It was all sounding terrific until Sally admitted that some men were responding a bit too much to her, especially at work. One colleague, she told us, even asked her out. Sally said that she was unaware of actually flirting, although by her own admission she was having fun practicing the sex appeal techniques she had learned. So she rightly asked, as many of our clients do at this point, just how much sex appeal is the right amount . . . especially at work. We were prepared. This is actually a hot topic, and a confusing one as well. For this last session, we met Sally after work, and she was dressed in a business suit with a skirt.

Research shows that the reason is that men view women's behavior very differently than women intend it. "So while a very sexy walk may make a woman feel more confident, it will make a man think right away about sex," I told Sally. "Even trickier is the fact that while women may be having fun by being what they consider just a little flirtatious, men often view the same behaviors as invitations for dating or sex. It's the gender-gap thing revisited."

"What's the answer then?" Sally asked.

"It really involves understanding how men interpret

women's behavior and adjusting their behavior for the right result," Stan told her. "That means a few things. Women need to tone down or eliminate the sexiest and most flirtatious behaviors in certain situations, including the workplace. They need to be very careful when engaging in fun, flirtatious behaviors and learn to engage in a method of mild flirtation, not seriously suggesting romantic interest, that is fun but should be clear to men in intention. They also need to learn certain power signals so that their approachability isn't perceived as excessive vulnerability."

"It sounds as if you're saying that after practicing turning up the volume on sexy behaviors, I have to learn to turn them down."

"That's right," Stan went on. "Especially in a work situation, you want to play up the gender signals that communicate approachability and confidence and play down the gender signals that communicate vulnerability and interest in sex. You are also going to want to incorporate certain power signals that will make you appear more confident and authoritative without compromising your femininity."

"That makes sense."

"There's actually a lot of good news here," Stan continued. "Did you know that women managers are generally judged more positively than male managers in most areas such as multitasking, delegating, and prioritizing? And they are rated particularly high on communication skills such as listening, handling and resolving conflicts, and mentoring. It seems that traditional female roles translate into better skills on the job."

"That's interesting. So it's not about not having sex appeal

Women Just Want to Have Fun (When Flirting)

In a study by David Lenningsen in the journal *Sex Roles* (2004), men and women were asked individually to imagine a situation of cross-sex flirting, write a script for what they think would happen, and describe the motivations likely to be involved.

Both men and women thought flirting was sometimes used to get attention and explore interest, whether sexual or not.

Men were about one-and-a-half times more likely to assume sexual interest was involved.

Women, on the other hand, at about the same ratio, were more likely to assume that the flirting was done for fun, for simple enjoyment.

Although it is likely that men are more inclined to think about sex when flirting, a possible explanation for these results is that men and women imagined different *types* of flirting. Men think of situations where serious romantic interest was conveyed, and women think of messages that were less serious and more casual in meaning.

at work, but just emphasizing certain elements of it while deemphasizing others?"

"Yes," Stan replied, "plus adding certain power signals to your repertoire. Let's talk about the effective use of gender signals first. If you want to communicate approachability and confidence but underplay vulnerability and interest in sex, how do you think you would do that?"

Sally thought for a minute. "I would probably eliminate the sexiest gender signals, like lip-licking, but still use signals that communicate some appeal."

"Good. Now let's review for a moment so that you can see how that translates into behavior. What do you think would be an appealing but not inappropriately sexy way of sitting?"

Sally shifted her position a few times, replaying the various behaviors she had learned. "Insinuating into the chair is pretty sexy, so I definitely wouldn't do that. I would imagine that good posture is important . . . always. I suppose that if I were wearing slacks, I'd be inclined to sit with my legs crossed, but not with one knee perched over the other. If I were wearing a skirt, I'd be conscious about it hiking up, so I'd probably sit with my legs to the side and my ankles crossed."

"You're opting for a moderate amount of sex appeal, and it definitely works in most situations," Stan said. "Occasionally, though, you might find yourself in a situation that is more conservative, so you would want to turn the volume down even lower by sitting with your legs in front of you and crossed at the ankle or with your legs together very slightly to the side. It looks a little more proper."

Rather sexy but still professional leg position.

Conservative but still sexy leg position.

Seven Days to Sex Appeal

"Most of the people I work with are young, so that probably wouldn't be necessary, but I'll keep that in mind for the future," Sally said.

"Let's take it to the next level," I said. "The way you are sitting is fine in general. But what if you were in a meeting and wanted to talk?"

"I would lean in."

"Good. How far?"

Sally became flustered. "I have no idea."

"How far you would lean in depends on the situation. For instance, if you are sitting in your boss's office and he or she is behind the desk, you might lean up to a foot. You would start from an erect position. Research shows that higher-status people generally relax more than subordinates, so an erect posture is polite with your boss. If you are with a coworker, however, and assuming that there is not a physical barrier like a desk between you, you might not need to lean in at all, unless the coworker is making it hard for you to speak. Generally, in a one-on-one situation with your boss or a coworker, the tactic of leaning forward while also nodding rapidly should only be used if you're having trouble getting into the conversation."

"What about where I should sit? Often there is more than one option."

"That's a great question," I said. "Choosing the most effective seat is important. It depends in part on whose office you are in, yours or the colleague's, and whether the other person is higher, lower, or equal in status to you. If it's your office, because women are better communicators and you want to play to your strong suit, I recommend not sitting behind a desk so that when you turn away from your desk, you have no barrier between you."

Sally said, "I have only a cubicle now, but I expect to have a regular office as soon as I'm promoted."

"Whether or not you have an office is not relevant," I continued. "If you're meeting with a colleague and he or she is behind a desk, it's a power trip. The best idea is to suggest moving to a different location for a discussion. At the very least, if there is a chair at the side of the desk, select that. Just remember, home territory gives the owner more power. Especially in a case of a likely conflict with a coworker, or even a boss, secure a neutral location for talk if at all possible."

"Where should I sit in my boss's office?"

"It depends on the options you're given," I told her. "If there is a seat on the side of the desk rather than in front of it, select that, although the boss might wave you toward one seat or the other."

"Where would be the best place to sit at a meeting?"

"Does your work group have meetings around a large table?" Stan asked.

"Yes, and our manager sits at one of the long ends of the table."

"And where do you sit?"

"Well, I usually sit at one the far corners from the boss's position because it feels safer."

"What would be the ideal position if you want to be heard when you speak?" Stan asked.

"I would never sit at the opposite end from the boss, because that might seem to challenge her position. But otherwise, I think the best spot is somewhere around the middle of one side or the other."

"Right," Stan said, "because from that position you can make eye contact readily with more people."

"What do you think would be the right amount of sex appeal when you stand?" I asked, continuing along.

Sally again tried various positions attempting to get a feel for what would be appealing but not over the top. "I can see that any stance with my pelvis or breasts thrust forward would be out of line. But I think that standing with my hand on my hip would be OK, with my feet together and one knee forward."

"That would be OK, but not as powerful as it could be," I said. "If you stand with your feet apart and one foot angled away, you will look more formidable and more balanced."

"Like I have both feet firmly planted on the ground!" Sally said, getting it. "So I guess I wouldn't tilt my ankle in either, for the same reason."

"That's right. It's too sexy and too vulnerable looking. Remember, you are trying to play down vulnerability also. That's why standing with your hands behind your back isn't a particularly effective stance either. It's not super sexy, but it looks too girly."

"And how would the way I stand change depending on whom I am talking to?"

"For the most part, any of these stances is OK regardless of whom you are talking to," I went on, "and you're not going to have the same stance all the time. The stance with feet apart and foot

A professional, sexy stance: one knee forward, hand on hip, thumb in front.

More powerful but less sexy professional stance: one foot angled away, hand on hip, thumb in back.

angled outward is the most powerful one. With your boss, you might want to use the less assertive stance with hand on hip and weight slightly off one foot. And you can turn it down more by not placing the hand on the hip, leaving your hands free to gesture."

"Then am I right to guess that the right walk would be some hip sway with erect posture?"

"You are right," Stan said. "You still want to look feminine and sexy, but not in an obvious or seductive way. And don't underestimate the importance of good posture in communicating confidence and overall attractiveness."

"That's the walk I've been using, so I don't have to change it. That's one less thing to think about."

"Another thing you probably won't have to think about is how you use your hands," Stan added. "Obviously you will not want to do any kind of self-touching that is sensual. However, everything you learned about gesturing by curving your wrists and splaying your fingers works at work. It's even OK to preen, but that should be very occasional. We would also suggest that you continue handling props such as eyeglasses or pencils in a feminine way."

"What about the handshake and waving hello or goodbye?" Sally asked.

"For the most part, a business handshake should be palm to palm," I told her. "Simply extending your hand with the palm down will come across as too vulnerable. When you wave, it's fine to splay and move your hand from side to side, but I wouldn't move your fingers individually. That looks too coy and girlish."

"OK," Sally continued. "Now let me guess about the next

thing we worked on: the use of the eyes. I would say that good eye contact is crucial. But you probably would not want to do any other gender signals like eye batting or sidelong glance."

"Actually, how to use your eyes at work is a bit more complicated than you might think," Stan said. "You're absolutely right that you do not want to bat your eyes, do a sidelong glance, face caress, or 'The Look,' which can look too seductive. But it's OK to do some eye fluttering in casual situations where you want to look a bit softer. Also, a quick room scan, when done in a large group during a social hour or just after a meeting, is engaging and shows you are open to approach, and it can also be used to signal specific people that you would like to speak to them. And it's obviously important to show good listening signals. For example, if you were talking to an employee about a personal problem and you want to be especially supportive, you would show *sad eyes*, with the brows knitted together above the eyes, while maintaining pretty constant eye contact. A slight head tilt and closed-mouth smile would be fitting as well."

"So when exactly shouldn't I maintain good eye contact?"

"When you're going to disagree or you're in a conflict situation, you can withdraw eye contact part of the time and discontinue nodding until you are ready to respond," Stan said.

"Isn't that kind of aggressive and unfeminine?" Sally asked.

"No. It's a sort of a polite way of warning the other person that you're not accepting everything he or she is saying," Stan responded. "Otherwise, if your body language could be interpreted as saying that you are in agreement with everything the other person is saying, the disagreement will come as an unpleasant surprise. And in the group situation, especially a large group, if you're going to disagree, you will need to maintain a certain amount of intermittent eye contact in order to get the speaker's attention, not nodding constantly but doing the rapid nodding just before beginning to express disagreement. In most other situations, however, good eye contact is important, especially since research shows that women tend to maintain more eye contact than men, so it's more expected of women."

"Remember," I explained, "you don't have to do everything women usually do, like listening intently all the time. It's the gender signals that remind others that you are feminine and approachable, even when you're disagreeing."

Sally became quiet for a moment. "If eye contact is not always good, then I would guess that smiling is also not always good."

"You would be guessing right," Stan said. "Research shows that women smile more often than men."

Sally got defensive. "So are you saying that at work, I should not smile any more than the men do?"

"No," I interjected. "You should smile more than men, because it's one of your assets—being approachable. But you should be selective in your smiling. Smile when you greet or say goodbye to someone, when receiving an appropriate compliment or responding to a funny remark, or when passing someone in the hall you've seen around but don't know well."

"The manner of smiling matters, too," Stan added. "For example, you should avoid frequent head tilting when smiling. It's OK sometimes for greetings, but it should be only a slight shift of

Getting and Keeping the Floor

Research by communication scholars Wiemann and Knapp (*Journal of Communication*, 1975) has shown that there are a number of behaviors that people can use to request the floor in a group, and the more signals you send, usually in the following order, the better your chances of being heard: (1) leaning forward; (2) direct eye contact to speaker, with rapid nodding; (3) hand position preparatory to gesture (usually hand on chin); (4) midair gesture before speaking; (5) audible inhalation of breath or "stutter starts" ("I . . . I . . . I . . . "); and (6) if absolutely necessary in a group where there is a lot of interrupting, speaking over another speaker's voice with increasing volume.

Finally, once you do get in, sociologist Starkey Duncan's research shows that even when you are pausing, you can keep the floor by using *turn-suppressing cues* such as vocal channel fillers, like "ahhhh" or "uhhhh" sounds, or continuing a midair gesture. (See *Journal of Personality and Social Psychology*, 1972.)

the head to one side, and it shouldn't be sustained for long, since research shows that's a very submissive behavior."

"Like exposing your jugular vein?" Sally asked.

"Precisely. And shifting your head from side to side while smiling, like a bobble-head toy, looks too submissive or ingratiating."

"So when shouldn't I smile?"

"Whenever you are in a conflict situation or where there is disagreement, as well as when you are trying to get into a conversation," I responded. "Imagine that you, Stan, and I are at a meeting. Stan and I will be talking to each other, and you should try to break in at some point. I'll turn on the video recorder so that we can replay it."

"I really think that there is way too much work for the present staff," Stan said, beginning to role-play. "We're all getting overworked, and our productivity is declining."

"I agree," I said. "But there is no room in the budget for more employees at the moment, so there's not much that can be done on that front."

We went back and forth for a minute, and then Sally leaned in, as we had suggested earlier, and began to speak.

"I think that . . ." was all she could get out before Stan interrupted her, barely acknowledging her presence before he began talking to me again. Then he turned to Sally. "Do you know what you just did?"

"I leaned in like you told me, but you ignored me."

"Let's watch the tape," I suggested. "What do you notice you did when you tried to speak?"

"I looked a little tentative when I leaned forward. Maybe I could have started to gesture."

"That's true, but what else did you do? Let's look at it again."

"Oh, you mean I smiled when I was trying to get in? I was just trying to show I wasn't disagreeing and was making a friendly suggestion."

"That's the problem," Stan said. "The smile contradicts your purpose because when you're trying to be assertive in getting into the talk, a smile communicates submissiveness, so other people know you won't press further to be heard. Research by communication scholar Carl Camden has shown that a smiling woman trying to get heard will likely be ignored by others, especially men."

"So I guess that's one time not to smile," Sally said.

"That's right, and you should leave out other friendly but submissive behaviors like a head tilt."

"What about if it's just casual, not a business meeting?"

"You can smile a lot more," I said, "and you may not have to be as forceful in getting into conversations, but you still want to have your share of the floor. It's good for your reputation."

We rehearsed having Sally get into the conversation a few more times until she was more forceful and had eliminated the smile. Sally went on to make the point that she felt was relevant, but after she had been speaking a bit, Stan interrupted her.

"That's much better," Stan said. "I think you'll notice a big difference in how much attention you command at meetings. There's one additional thing that would help, though. You speak a bit too slowly. When making a presentation or even when talking in a group, it's more effective to use a fairly fast rate of speaking—not so fast as to leave people out, obviously. And you should also use quite a few gestures, brief eye contact with each listener, one at a time, and a good deal of vocal variety to emphasize your points."

"It sounds like you're saying I'm not animated enough."

"Yes, you need to work on that a bit. The way you are using your voice would be fine in one-on-one business conversations where it's more effective to use somewhat less vocal variety and gestures."

"Another thing to keep in mind is that in one-on-one conversations, you want to practice vocal matching," I said, "although don't match immediately, since it's submissive and you want to see if others will match your pace. Pace and lead with people who are too slow by starting slow to match and then gradually going faster. On the other hand, with people who are too fast, match their pace first, and then see if you can slow them down."

"Sort of like what you do with flirting, right?"

"Yes, although vocal matching is useful in almost any conversation if you want the person to feel you are in sync with them."

"What do you think about the pitch of my voice?" Sally asked.

"It's fine. You're at a pretty optimum level of pitch, and it is much more relaxed than it used to be, so it doesn't sound so squeaky. Why are you asking?" I said.

"There's a woman at work who uses this high-pitched little girl voice, especially when dealing with older males in senior management positions. And they seem to respond well to her. But from what you've told me, that shouldn't be effective."

"I've had female students do that to me," Stan said. "It's done to try and bring out an older male's paternalistic impulses. There is the rare female who is extremely powerful in other ways who can get away with it. But for the most part it makes you seem weak and vulnerable and is a risky strategy. So I would definitely avoid it. And it's especially too vulnerable when accompanied with wide-open eyes."

"Let's see if I've got it so far," Sally said. "Smiling is good because it makes me seem more approachable, but I shouldn't do submissive signals with smiles, except maybe a quick head tilt for a friendly greeting, and I shouldn't smile when trying to take a turn, especially in a group."

"Very good!" Stan and I said in unison.

"A quick room scan can be good when I enter the room," she continued. "And I should position myself in a group where I can see and be seen and use as many *turn requesting* signals as needed to be able to speak. When I speak in a large group, I should use a slightly faster speed, and in one-on-one interactions, I should focus more on matching the pace. When I'm listening, I should maintain good eye contact except in situations of conflict and disagreement."

"Very good—you're a good student!" I said. "You're ready to tackle the big one . . . how to successfully flirt at work. As I said before, women are more likely to see flirting as fun, and men tend to see flirting as more sexual. An article in the *Wall Street Journal* on February 7, 2000, noted that women, especially young women, are being more outgoing in their behavior, and some female consultants actually recommend using your attractiveness on the job. So the bottom line is that you can flirt at times on the job but you have to do it in a very specific way so that men don't get the wrong idea. In 1965, the nonverbal expert Albert Scheflen called it *quasi-courtship*."

"Quasi-what?"

"Quasi-courtship is a technical term that simply means you are flirting but with signals that qualify the flirting so that it is clear that you're just having fun," I explained. "It's a way of saying, 'You're attractive, or you're fun to flirt with, but I'm not romantically interested.'"

"In other words, let's play but don't expect sex."

"Pretty much. The good news about quasi-courtship is that it makes casual conversations more interesting, helps salespeople make sales, and comes across as extra-friendly and a boost to the person's ego you're doing it with. But there are rules that you absolutely must follow if you don't want to give the wrong impression."

"Such as . . . ?"

"Obviously, any of the hot flirtatious stuff such as lip-licking or any kind of touch including sensually touching yourself are out. Some courting signals like preening, head tilting, even some eye fluttering or wide-open eyes are OK, but not the most sexy stances."

"I'm not that bad a student!" Sally said. "I think I figured that out myself."

"I know. Just wanted to mention it. But it's the qualifiers that make it clear that the flirting is not serious. Actually, the situation itself can help to qualify the flirting signals, especially when you're in an office and there are other people nearby. It reinforces the impression that you are not doing something illicit or private."

"Oops. I definitely screwed that one up," Sally said. "Remember the guy I was telling you about who asked me out? Well, I was doing some mild flirtation at the company picnic, and while there were people around, we were standing off to the side."

"That situation is a little ambiguous because you were away from the office," Stan said. "But what is really important is that you send clear body language signals. You can call attention to the fact that the situation is inappropriate for serious flirting by glancing around from time to time, as if to say 'Notice where we are.' Even at the picnic, if you had looked over at the other people nearby several times, he should begin to get the message."

"Drawing subtle attention to the surroundings is especially useful as a qualifier at work," I added. "But there are also other signals you can send—the more signals, the clearer the intention."

"Such as?"

"The most important thing is to keep your body oriented somewhat away from the guy. Remember how you learned that as courtship progresses, people turn more and more toward each other? By standing off somewhat to the side, things will appear as if they are not progressing anywhere."

"In other words, I'm interrupting the courtship sequence," Sally said.

"That's right—good insight," I responded.

"Actually," Sally said, "I can't remember whether I was

oriented away from the guy, but I do think I was standing a little too close, maybe about a foot and a half away."

"What Edward Hall, in 1966, called the intimate zone," Stan said, nodding in affirmation. "Yes, that's too close. And one of the things about the courtship sequence is that people not only gradually turn their bodies more toward one another, but they also move in closer."

"There are some other qualifiers to use to clarify your intentions," I added. "For example, you could look at another male passing by. It's like saying, 'I'm not just focusing on you.'"

"I've had guys do that to me, looking at another female, when I'm actually on a date!" Sally said. "And you're right. It doesn't take a genius to know that is not a good sign as far as interest goes. Are there any other things I should be aware of to not come across as too flirty?"

"This one you probably know," I told her, "so don't be insulted. It is always a good idea to qualify flirty behavior with a coworker by mentioning a boyfriend or date or husband or children."

"Yeah, I know that one. The thing is that I don't have a boyfriend right now, and I don't want to lie."

"Not a problem," says Stan. "Talk about someone you're dating. Or as a more gentle solution, shift the topic to less personal things. Talk about work, or if you're about ready to depart, talk about work you need to get back to. You can accompany this with other leave-taking signals—looking away more often, shuffling your feet as if to go somewhere, even saying things like 'It was really nice talking to you.'"

"Won't guys get insulted by all these put-off messages?"

"No," Stan said, "most guys will appreciate the attention and the message that they're attractive, even though you're not into romance."

"And there will be a few guys who just don't get it," I reminded her. "Some guys even think that if a woman smiles at them, she's interested. It's called 'desperation.'" Everybody laughed.

"Let's try practicing quasi-courtship," I suggested. "Imagine Stan is a colleague at work, you haven't seen him for a while, and you're pausing for a few minutes in the hall to talk."

Sally stood facing Stan almost head-on. "Hi, Stan, I haven't seen you in a while," Sally said, smiling, tilting her head, and preening a couple of times.

"Boy, am I glad to see you," Stan said, smiling too broadly and preening.

Sally stopped the role-play. "What did I do to get that response?"

"A few things," Stan told her. "You are standing pretty close to me and head-on. You're also being too coy by tilting your head and preening. It really does look like you are flirting for real."

"Let's try it once more," I suggested.

Sally started the conversation again, without facing Stan head-on. She smiled but preened less. Stan spoke about his week at tennis camp. Sally said that tennis was always something she wanted to learn to play, but even the guy she was dating had given up on teaching her. As they continued talking, she looked around the office from time to time. She was doing really well

Author Stan and Sally Role-play a Conversation at the Office

Position is too flirty.

A slight change in position turns down the sex appeal.

when Stan decided to throw in a curve ball to see how she would handle it.

"I'd love to have the chance to teach you how to play," Stan said, grinning.

Sally stopped abruptly. "What I am doing wrong now?" she asked. "I remembered to avoid moving more directly or close to him, I looked around as if to suggest that I was not interested just in him, and I even let him know I am dating someone. And he still came on to me!"

"You were actually doing well. I just wanted to test you," Stan said. "In a real situation like this, you would want to not do any more flirting signals with him. Hopefully, he'll get the message. If he persists, you tell him you're not interested. If he keeps insisting, you can warn him first, and later report him for sexual harassment if necessary. Just be sure you are giving clear signals. The opposite side of the coin is that some women think they are only flirting casually, but they don't do the qualifying signals."

"I get it," Sally said. "But with all of this, what if I really do like the guy—I mean, what if I would be interested in dating him?"

"Office romances do happen, and they are more and more common, and there is a certain amount of acceptance of them in some organizations," I said. "If you want to explore this possibility, meet him out of the office environment."

"And once you've done that," Stan said, "I recommend continuing to do quasi-courtship with him and even with others when you're in the office. It's tricky—you don't want to change your behavior radically in the workplace because it will call attention to your budding relationship."

"What if I do get romantically involved with someone from the place where I work, hypothetically speaking?" Sally asked.

"Then you don't show it in observable ways," Stan replied. "You don't hold hands, put your arms around each other, or whisper something in the other person's ear while others are around. Not even as you're going out to the parking lot at the end of the day. You have to be off corporate grounds."

"Won't other people know?" Sally asked.

"It doesn't matter!" we said in unison. "Just don't display it!"

"This has been really informative," Sally told us. "I can see how important it is to communicate the right amount of sex appeal at work, and depending on how you do it, it can either help or hurt. Is there anything else I need to know?"

"Actually, we teach a whole course on 'Charisma Coaching.' It is basically about everything you need to know to have people perceive you as charismatic."

"At work?" Sally asked, her curiosity piqued.

"No, everywhere," I told her. "But that's for another time. You have plenty to work on now."

"So are we done?"

"For now we are," Stan said, "although before we leave today, Eva and I would like some feedback about this experience."

Sally thought for a while. "It's really been powerful—life changing, actually. It was very, very tough at first. I guess no one really likes to see how they appear to other people. And it was disheartening to see how many things I had to correct just to have some semblance of sex appeal. But the longer we went on, the easier it became. I was less self-conscious over time. Also, as I started to see that it actually works and began to get better responses from the opposite sex, it became fun! I know I have a lot more to practice, but I feel that I have all the basic tools I need."

"It takes anywhere from a few weeks to a few months of practicing these skills regularly before you develop muscle memory and they become a natural part of your nonverbal repertoire," I told her. "But with time and practice, pretty much anyone can develop sex appeal."

"Well, you guys both have it," Sally said, laughing.

"It's not an age, but an attitude," Stan said, winking.

"Get back to us every once in a while," I said. "We like to hear from clients."

"I will for sure," Sally said. And she gave each of us a hug.